FOREWORD

Pete MacDonald from the Friends of the Moray Firth Dolphins explains why Britain has some of the best whale and dolphin watching in Europe

C all me superstitious if you like, but after years of watching cetaceans (whales, dolphins, and porpoises), I am convinced that the best way to spot them is by not looking! That's the way it always seems to happen. You are standing on a cliff edge or on a beach, or perhaps out on the water with a wildlife cruise boat, and for the past few hours you have seen nothing. So you set off home or to your holiday accommodation and what happens? You hear about an amazing sighting seconds after you stopped watching the water! Cetaceans, don't you just love them? They are so unpredictable!

But whilst this might sound frustrating (and often is), it is also what makes watching whales and dolphins in the wild so exciting. And, for me, the true place to see these magnificent animals is in the wild. No aquarium can compare to watching cetaceans free and in their natural habitat, with Britain's fabulous coastline, ever-changing weather and people as the backdrop.

The coastline of Great Britain has some of the best cetacean watching sites in Europe, with regular sightings of Common Bottlenose Dolphins, Harbour Porpoises and Northern Minke Whales, not to mention any one of the 25 other species that have been seen in our waters or have stranded dead on our shores. In Britain you are never more than 72 miles away from the sea, and a potential encounter with a cetacean. Whether you are in Scotland, Wales, or England, this book will tell you all you need to know about how and where to look, and how to interpret what you find. So if you would like to have a spectacular whale or dolphin encounter without leaving our shores, I thoroughly recommend that you have this book by your side on your travels, no matter where you live in Great Britain.

Pete MacDonald

Moray Firth dolphins © Pete McDonald

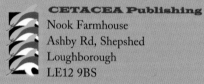

Authors: Dylan Walker and Alex Wilson

First published 2007 by Cetacea Publishing

CETACEA Publishing
Nook Farmhouse
Ashby Rd, Shepshed
Loughborough
LE12 9BS

Telephone: +44 (0) 845 388 3053
Fax: +44 (0) 845 108 6386

E-mail: info@CetaceaPublishing.com
Website: www.CetaceaPublishing.com

Editor: Sue Cameron

Webmaster: Matt Wildman

Design / Website: deZilver, www.dezilver.com

Front cover: Cardigan Bay, Common
Bottlenose Dolphins, *photograph Steve Hartley*

ISBN-10: 0-9556144-0-6
ISBN-13: 978-0-9556144-0-8

The publishers would like to thank the following organisations for their support in the production of this book

Whale and Dolphin Conservation Society

CONTENTS

INTRODUCTION

Anybody who has had a close encounter with one of the world's big predators will have experienced a feeling of overwhelming primeval fear and awe, writes *Dylan Walker*. Big cats, wolves, bears, and sharks are animals that command our greatest respect as powerful and accomplished hunters.

You would think that we are safe from such emotions in Britain. By 1700 we had eradicated both Wolves and Brown Bears from the British countryside, and our biggest shark, the Basking Shark, eats only plankton. Imagine my surprise then, when on one fateful June day, whilst visiting the magical Shetland Islands in the far north of Scotland, I came face to face with an animal that weighs in at over nine tonnes – the equivalent of a small tank, and bares a set of ferocious teeth. I found myself frozen to the spot with my stomach in knots and my eyes watering. Two enormous bull Killer Whales were heading straight for me!

These Killer Whales (otherwise known as Orcas) were moving quickly. Their enormous dorsal fins knifed through the water effortlessly. Their heads launched through the waves to reveal ominous, dinner-plate-sized white eye patches. Finally, their broad backs rolled forward, all rippling muscle and hydrodynamic efficiency. My heart was racing, my hands were shaking, and my spine was tingling.

How close would they come? When would they alter course? Finally, just 10m away, they swept to the right, turning broadside whilst emitting high misty blows that hung in the air in front of me. As they left the scene I realised that I had forgotten to keep breathing, and immediately took a sharp intake of air. I knew it was one of the most incredible wildlife experiences of my life. Not only had I encountered the most powerful predator in the ocean from our shores, I hadn't even left the shore to do it!

With both feet firmly planted on dry land, I couldn't have been safer, and yet I had almost been within touching distance of these magnificent and intelligent mammals. I sat back on the rocks to gather my thoughts. In time, I realised what they were up to. Each summer, small groups of Killer Whales return to the islands to prey upon Common and Atlantic Grey Seals, often approaching close to shore in the hope of a surprise attack. On this occasion, they were not successful. Every seal in the vicinity had edged beyond the high tide line. The Killer Whales were out of luck, but I felt like the luckiest person on earth!

Watching Killer Whales in Shetland © hughharrop.com

We wrote this book, explains *Alex Wilson*, for anybody who would like to have an incredible encounter like that described on the previous page. *Whales and Dolphins of Great Britain* illustrates that, far from being a 'freak event', such encounters are commonplace around our coastline, with numerous opportunities to see cetaceans in locations spread the length and breadth of the country.

Whales and Dolphins of Great Britain is the first comprehensive guide to the whales, dolphins and porpoises of British waters. Not only are all of the regularly seen species described in detail, there is also concise information on where to see them from land, from whale and dolphin watching boats and from ferries. The text gives all of the information required for the reader to book a trip, which species are likely to be seen, how to get there and what photographic opportunities exist. The result is a unique guide for anybody with an interest in cetaceans and whale and dolphin watching. It is our hope that this book will, by bringing together a wealth of information in a format which will appeal to both beginner and expert, also attract people who had no idea that they could go whale watching from our shores. We hope you enjoy whale and dolphin watching in Great Britain as much as we have. It really is a uniquely wonderful place!

Photography:
below, Humpback Whale ©Alex Wilson / WildPics.org,
right, Common Bottlenose Dolphin © Pete MacDonald

OUR THANKS

It would be fair to say that we have been overwhelmed by the positive feedback and offers of assistance in the production of this book. Without the help of so many people across Britain, only a few of which can be named below, this project simply would not have been possible.

The authors would particularly like to thank the many whale watch businesses, advertisers, and conservation organisations that have provided information for this book. In particular, the text has been reviewed by key local and

national experts, including Richard Baines, Debbie Benham, Graeme Cresswell, Ian Broadbent, Fran and Chris Cree, Lisa Gorman, Hugh Harrop, Dan Jarvis, Ruth Leeney, Kelly MacLeod, Stephen Marsh, Fiona Quarmby, Nigel Scott, and David Tipping.

Thanks also to the outstanding photographers that provided such excellent images of the places and animals not photographed by the authors. In particular, we would like to thank Richard Baines, Stephen Berry, Ian Broadbent, Alex Carlisle, Graeme Cresswell, Toni Cross, Hugh Harrop, Steve Hartley, Dan Jarvis, Sarah Perry, Charlie Phillips and John Young.

We are also very grateful for the expert opinions of Margaux Dodds, Liz Sandeman, Steve Hartley, Greg Kauffman, Fiona Manson, Colin Speedy, Peter Stevick, and Vanessa Williams-Grey on the subject of responsible whale watching. Meanwhile, Pete MacDonald kindly provided us with an excellent foreword. A special thanks also goes to Matt Wildman for setting up the Cetacea Publishing website. Finally, Alex would like to thank Wally and Trish Franklin, Vic Cockcroft and Debbie Young for inspiring his passion for whales and dolphins.

Introduction

Join an Earthwatch research project and you will be playing your part in whale and dolphin conservation.

Don't just
watch whales...
...help us to help them.

Dolphins and whales face increasing threats from fisheries, coastal development, habitat disturbance and pollution.

Here at Earthwatch we are doing everything we can to understand these threats and determine the key to their long-term survival. Why not volunteer on one of our research teams and help scientists collect crucial data which contributes to the protection of these cetaceans?

On our research project *Whales and Dolphins of Moray Firth* in Scotland, for example, you would learn to identify minke whales, bottlenose dolphins and harbour porpoises, recording data such as composition of groups, geographic position and behaviour.

Our long-term research would be impossible without our teams of dedicated volunteers. You don't need special skills or experience – you just need to be 18 or over.

Your project cost includes:
• All accommodation and food
• Comprehensive briefing materials
• Training in the field
• Emergency medical evacuation if necessary

Earthwatch is an international environmental charity supporting 130 research projects around the world. As well as our UK-based research, we support whale and dolphin projects in Europe, the Americas and New Zealand.

Since Earthwatch was founded in 1971, our scientists and volunteers have achieved amazing results for conservation, including the creation of national parks and the discovery of new species. For instance, as a direct result of research carried out on our *Spanish Dolphins* project, the International Maritime Organisation agreed to divert shipping lanes off the southern coast of Spain by 20 miles to avoid important bottlenose dolphin foraging grounds.

Images © Dr Kevin Robinson; Karen Alcock; Sarah Staunton Lamb

Take action today. Help us to make a difference. Call **+44 (0)1865 318831**, or visit **www.earthwatch.org** for a full range of projects.

WHAT IS A CETACEAN?

Throughout this book there are references to the word 'cetacean',
but what does the word mean and what are cetaceans?

All whales, dolphins, and porpoises belong to an Order of marine mammals called Cetacea, and are collectively known as cetaceans. Like other mammals, cetaceans are warm-blooded, breathe air through their lungs and suckle their young. However, unlike most other mammals, cetaceans live exclusively in water. Their adaptations for life in the oceans are so advanced that many cetaceans superficially resemble fish, particularly sharks, in form and structure. One of the best ways of differentiating a cetacean from a fish is by looking at the orientation of the tail: horizontal in cetaceans, vertical in fish.

There are currently 86 recognised species within the Order Cetacea. Of these, an amazing 28 species have been recorded in British waters. The cetaceans are divided into two groups or Sub-orders: the Mysticeti or baleen whales, and the Odontoceti or toothed cetaceans.

In Europe, baleen whales range in size from the Northern Minke Whale, which rarely reaches 10m in length, to the massive Blue Whale, which grows to over 30m. Instead of teeth, these whales have plates of baleen (whalebone), which hang from the roof of their mouths. These vertical plates can grow to over 2m in length in some species and are used to filter enormous quantities of small fish and crustaceans. Baleen whales can also be distinguished because they have two external nostrils or blowholes.

The European species of toothed cetacean range in size from the huge Sperm Whale, with a maximum length of 18m, to the tiny Harbour Porpoise, which reaches a maximum length of just 1.8m. Toothed cetaceans hunt agile fish and squid and, like bats, are able to locate their prey using sonar. Besides having teeth, the Odontoceti are distinguished by having only one external nostril or blowhole. Seventy two species of toothed cetacean are currently recognised, the smallest of which are generally known as dolphins or porpoises.

The following diagrams illustrate the main differences between the baleen whales and the toothed cetaceans, and give the names of the key external body parts that can be important in identification at sea.

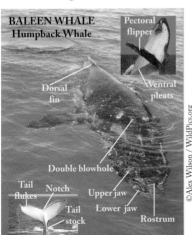

BALEEN WHALE
Humpback Whale
Pectoral flipper
Dorsal fin
Ventral pleats
Double blowhole
Tail flukes
Notch
Tail stock
Upper jaw
Lower jaw
Rostrum

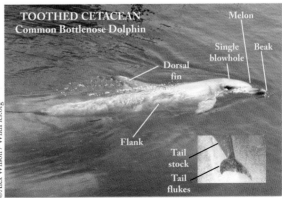

TOOTHED CETACEAN
Common Bottlenose Dolphin
Melon
Single blowhole
Beak
Dorsal fin
Flank
Tail stock
Tail flukes

© Alex Wilson / WildPics.org

Photographs, left and above, show the main differences between baleen whales and toothed cetaceans, and give the names of the key external body parts useful for identification. Note the photographs are not shown to scale.

WDCS
Whale and Dolphin Conservation Society

WILDLIFE centre

The WDCS Wildlife Centre is owned and operated by WDCS, the Whale and Dolphin Conservation Society.

Beautifully situated at the mouth of the River Spey, the centre is housed in an eighteenth century former salmon fishing station.

The area has long been renowned for it's wildlife. Bottlenose dolphins visit the bay and delight visitors with their charismatic behaviour. Osprey, seals and otters may also be spotted around the mouth of the river.

Make our centre your first stop and enjoy our free exhibition, daily wildlife talks, cafe and gift shop.

The WDCS Wildlife Centre is located in north east Scotland, 5 miles from the A96, approximately 1 hour's drive from Inverness, Aberdeen and Aviemore.
Opening times: Easter to 30th October: 10.30am-5pm, 7 days a week. Please contact us for winter opening hours.

Contact us: WDCS Wildlife Centre, Spey Bay, Moray, IV32 7PJ, Scotland
Tel: 01343 820 339 **E-mail:** wildlifecentre@wdcs.org
Website: www.wdcs.org/wildlifecentre

GREAT BRITAIN

An outstanding place to go whale and dolphin watching

Introduction

The opportunities for watching whales and dolphins in Great Britain are as exciting as they are varied. This is not surprising when you consider that our islands consist of 9,040 miles of coastline overlooking the North Sea, English Channel, Irish Sea, Celtic Sea and westwards to the open Atlantic. Our sailing traditions give away Britain's impressive maritime location, being superbly situated at the western edge of the European continent and completely surrounded by water. Despite this, it is often assumed that whales and dolphins only exist far from our shores, in clear tropical waters or at the edge of the polar ice.

Nothing could be further from the truth. British waters play host to a plethora of whale, dolphin and porpoise species. Some, such as the Northern Minke Whale, Harbour Porpoise and Common Bottlenose Dolphin, are easily viewed from land or dedicated whale watching boats. Others, including the Long-finned Pilot Whale, White-beaked Dolphin and Killer Whale are present in certain locations at specific times. Finally, there are those species, such as the Humpback Whale, Fin Whale and Sperm Whale, that are capable of turning up almost anywhere, yet they are all only rarely sighted.

The really exciting thing about whale and dolphin watching in Britain is that in order to see all of the species above and more, you have to make the most of the many different opportunities that exist throughout our Isles for watching cetaceans. The most obvious of these is to take a trip with one of the many dedicated whale watch operators listed in this book. These boats are travelling further and seeing more species every year. But there is another, more adventurous side to whale watching in Great Britain. This involves taking a ferry, yacht, or other boat and simply going exploring, or picking a remote headland, taking your binoculars and telescope, and just waiting to see what happens. Whilst this might seem like a bit of a random thing to do, the truth is that we still have much to learn about the lives of cetaceans on our doorstep. Whilst you may see nothing as a result of your adventures, you may also have an encounter with a rare species or witness a behaviour that few people have ever seen in the wild before.

Dolphin on the bow © Charlie Phillips

Why Great Britain?

Want to see cetaceans and help their conservation at the same time?

GET INVOLVED at the sharp end of cetacean research!

Founded in 2000, the charity ORCA (Organisation Cetacea) has logged more than 35,000 animals to date, from harbour porpoises to rare blue whales, surveying over 45,000 kilometres on major ferry routes around Europe.

Working in an area stretching from the Bay of Biscay off northern Spain to the Norwegian Arctic, we aim to raise public awareness of marine mammals, encouraging public participation in their study via a volunteer network of trained observers.

ORCA routinely collects data and makes it available to students, research bodies, industry and governmental departments.  With marine life facing many threats including climate change, fisheries by-catch, chemical and acoustic pollution and over-fishing, the information we gather is vital for monitoring and safeguarding not just cetaceans, but the entire marine ecosystem.

Members of the Atlantic Research Coalition, we forge and promote data collection partnerships, working with like-minded bodies across the UK and Europe.

*A fee is charged for our training courses

YOU can help!

We need more volunteers to train* and take part in our surveys, but if your sea legs aren't that stable, you can still become involved in our charity work or offer financial support through donations. Whatever you can do to help, you'll be joining a team of dedicated individuals undertaking invaluable work to aid the conservation of cetaceans and our increasingly impoverished oceans.

To find out how to volunteer, register your interest in our forthcoming training days, or make a donation, please either email us at **enquiries@orcaweb.org.uk** or visit our website at

www.orcaweb.org.uk

Charity Number: 1098765

Beyond the surf

So why are the waters around Great Britain of such importance for cetaceans? The answer is that our seas offer a whole range of different oceanic conditions that provide distinct habitats for different species and populations. One of the most important factors is depth. Great Britain sits on the European continental shelf surrounded by relatively shallow seas that are generally less than 200m deep. Shallow waters are important for several species of cetacean that feed on or near the bottom, such as Harbour Porpoise, Common Bottlenose Dolphin and White-beaked Dolphin.

To the west of Great Britain, where the continental shelf drops away to the ocean floor, the water depth increases dramatically, reaching several thousand metres below sea level in some places. These waters run particularly close to the west and north of Scotland, and support deep-diving squid hunting cetaceans such as the Sperm Whale, Northern Bottlenose Whale and Long-finned Pilot Whale. The proximity of deep water also influences the frequency with which large baleen whales enter British waters. They are believed to follow the edge of the continental shelf on their annual migrations between Arctic feeding grounds and warm-water breeding grounds. However, every year, small numbers of Fin, Sei and Humpback Whales pass close to our shores, having apparently taken a detour from their main migration routes.

Current knowledge

British waters are also influenced by a number of major water currents. Some bring cold or warm water close to shore. Others carry important nutrients, whilst still others are partially desalinated by the great rivers of the British Isles and mainland Europe. One current that is so significant that it affects the climate of Europe, is the Gulf Stream. Originating near the Bahamas in the Caribbean, it sweeps north-east at a speed that can exceed 125km per day! Passing to the west of Britain, it has a significant warming effect on our seas, raising their temperatures above normal for this latitude, and providing suitable conditions for Risso's Dolphin, Short-beaked Common Dolphin and Common Bottlenose Dolphin, all of which prefer warm temperate waters. Indeed, Scotland's Moray Firth is home to the world's most northerly resident population of Bottlenose Dolphins.

Although we love to complain about it, the changeable nature of the British weather is actually an asset for our cetaceans! The gales that frequently whip up our seas during the winter months play an important role in mixing up water layers and dispersing nutrients. During the long summer days, planktonic organisms gather near the sea surface and convert these nutrients during photosynthesis. These phytoplankton form the basis of a marine food chain that ends with whales, dolphins and seabirds. So the combination of turbulent winter seas and long, calm, summer days provides for a productive marine ecosystem and an abundance of prey for whales and dolphins.

Getting back to nature

There are numerous factors that attract whales, dolphins, and porpoises to the seas around Britain. In turn, we have become so captivated by their grace, intelligence, and, in some cases, sheer size, that we are heading to the coast and out on the water in increasing numbers just to catch a glimpse of these magnificent mammals. In so doing, we remind ourselves of the importance and fragility of Britain's sea life, and the responsibility we all share if we are to preserve it for the future.

Acrobatic dolphins © Alex Wilson / WildPics.org

WHEN, WHERE AND HOW
to go whale and dolphin watching in Great Britain?
This chapter provides information on when, where and how to look for cetaceans, with details of the equipment required for a successful and enjoyable whale watching excursion.

When?

Although cetaceans spend much of their time underwater, they must return to the surface to breathe on a regular basis. The amount of time spent at the surface varies greatly from species to species and is also dependent upon whether the animal is resting, feeding or travelling. It is important to be patient when watching the water, as it could be some time before a cetacean pops up! Cetaceans are generally easier to find in some seasons than in others. Different species occur in different waters in different months, so the dedicated whale watcher is likely to encounter a greater diversity of species by watching in all seasons. It is widely accepted that in Great Britain summer is the best time to watch. There are several reasons for this: high-pressure weather systems often settle for considerable periods bringing warm, sunny and windless conditions; the sea is generally at its calmest; and day length is at its greatest, allowing more time for watching. As the summer progresses, these factors combine to increase water temperature, allowing phytoplankton (the 'green grass' of the marine ecosystem) to flourish. Warm, sunny conditions enable these free-floating marine plants to increase in numbers dramatically, providing food, either directly or indirectly, for all other marine creatures from microscopic zooplankton to mighty whales.

© Charlie Phillips

When, Where and How?

Where?

Cetaceans tend to be sparsely distributed and difficult to find. Like their predatory mammalian relatives on land, they are at or near the top of the food chain, occurring at low densities over large areas. Knowing where to look is therefore very important. Some cetaceans favour shallow waters or coastal areas, whereas others restrict themselves to very deep water. Some are resident, whilst others are migratory. Whilst water depth and oceanographic features can be useful indicators of the habitat of a particular species, location alone should not be used as a way of specifically identifying a cetacean. Part of the joy of watching cetaceans is their complete unpredictability. It is almost impossible to guess where they will occur because they can pop up anywhere at any time. Marine mammals do not follow any rules. They roam freely over great distances and there is still much to learn about their distribution and migratory patterns. For the whale watcher, the most important principle is to put in as much time as possible, as sooner or later such efforts will be rewarded.

How

When searching for whales and dolphins it is very important to choose a good place from which to watch. On land, the best locations are often headlands with a reasonably high vantage point, particularly those that extend to deep water. A good tip is to seek out lighthouses, which are often built on the most prominent headlands. Binoculars and often a telescope are useful tools for land-based watching. Most coastal area are visited by cetaceans occasionally, but some regions entertain a greater diversity and abundance of species than others At the very best locations it may be possible to see several species of dolphin and whale over the course of a year. Other sites are visited occasionally or seasonally. Land-based watching generally requires patience and concentration whilst scanning the sea systematically. Even at the most famous sites listed in this book, it is typical to spend significant periods of time – hours or even days – without a sighting.

However, there are ways in which you can maximize your chances of an encounter. Firstly, check the weather and choose a windless day to watch. Cetaceans are much more obvious in a calm sea, and visibility is also likely to be better. Secondly, binoculars and, preferably, a telescope, are essential tools for watching from a high cliff. With good optical equipment it is possible to have fantastic encounters with these animals, safe in the knowledge that you are not influencing their behaviour in any way, as you might from a boat. Finally, take sufficient supplies to enjoy the day. Make sure you have plenty of clothes to protect against all weathers, and take a picnic lunch. There are few more enjoyable experiences in life than watching dolphins playing, taking in fabulous scenery, and enjoying a cheese and pickle sandwich, all at the same time!

Whale and dolphin watchers using boats should also carry binoculars in order to get closer views of the animals. Reputable whale watching boat operators follow a code of conduct that will limit their ability to closely approach cetaceans in certain circumstances

© Dylan Walker / breathtakingwhales.com

(although it is often the cetaceans that approach the boats), so your binoculars can be invaluable. The bridge and close to the bow of the boat are good places from which to search, since this allows for observation ahead of the vessel. A stable platform is necessary in order to use binoculars without too much shake. Elevation is also an important consideration, particularly in rougher seas when a high vantage-point allows the observer to track cetaceans as they travel through wave troughs. Also consider gaining shelter from the wind, reducing glare from the sun and avoiding sea spray.

Finding cetaceans requires a great deal of patience. Keep searching over the same area of water even if you think there is nothing there. Some deep-water species can stay underwater for an hour or more before eventually surfacing. Watching cetaceans from a boat is generally easiest in relatively calm weather. A sea with few or no white caps to the waves is preferable, as whales and leaping dolphins are often first noticed because of the white water they create as they surge through the water's surface. Having observed an unusual splash, a possible blow or a dark shape in the water, check with your binoculars. It may be nothing but more often than not your first impressions will have been correct and you will have found a cetacean!

Equipment

The most important considerations for a successful day's whale watching at sea or from the coast are the bare essentials: warm dry clothes, food and water. Even if it is a hot calm day on land, weather conditions at sea can be deceptively cool and changeable. As a general rule try to dress for all weathers. Take several layers of clothing, which will improve insulation in cold weather and give you several options if it is warm. A warm hat will prevent around 35% of your body heat being lost through your head. Windproof or waterproof clothing is essential.

To avoid seasickness it is important to remain hydrated with a full stomach so take plenty of non-alcoholic drink and snack food with you. If you feel seasick, it can help to eat even if you don't feel like it. Much of a whale watching trip may be spent travelling to and from wildlife or scenic hotspots. You may wish to read a book, look for seabirds and other marine life or simply watch the sea. Whale watch operators will often ask for your help in searching for marine mammals, so why not start watching and gain some field experience. Apart from a good field guide, binoculars are the most essential piece of equipment for observing whales and dolphins. They can be used to scan the sea at distance, and they increase your chances of observing subtle behaviours or identification features that would go undetected with the naked eye. If possible, buy a good pair of binoculars that feel comfortable and are not too heavy, with a magnification of between 7x and 10x and a wide field of view. Telescopes (of the type typically used by birdwatchers) are very useful for land-based watching and can also be used on large, stable vessels. However, they are best used in conjunction with binoculars, which are generally more suitable for scanning the sea because they have a much wider field of view.

© breathtakingwhales.com

HARBOUR PORPOISE
Phocoena phocoena

Key identification features

Britain's smallest cetacean and the only species of porpoise. Easily identified because of its very small 1.5m length, low and triangular dorsal fin, small head lacking a beak, and inconspicuous movements. Body is dark grey, with the exception of the belly, which is white.

Behaviour

This timid cetacean is generally sighted alone or in small groups and tends to travel quite slowly, generally avoiding boats. Unlike dolphins, Harbour Porpoises are unobtrusive, making them very difficult to observe in rough seas. Usually surfaces leisurely three or four times before a dive of two to three minutes. Harbour Porpoises consume a range of schooling fish that occur in the water column or close to the sea floor, including Mackerel, Hake, Pollock and Whiting. However, in many parts of Great Britain, Herring is easily the most important prey species, making up between 50% and 80% of the diet.

Distribution and habitat

Restricted to the cold temperate to sub-arctic waters of the Northern Hemisphere, Harbour Porpoises prefer sea temperatures below 15ºC. They favour shallow waters inshore of 200m, especially coastal areas, including bays, headlands, and river mouths. The most widespread and abundant cetacean in Britain, despite having suffered marked declines in several regions. Important populations remain around mainland Scotland, the Western Isles and Northern Isles. Other strongholds include the southern Irish Sea, Cardigan Bay and the Western Approaches to the English Channel. Many populations have shown significant declines in the last 50 years, with a 95% decrease in Cornish sightings, whilst populations in parts of the southern North Sea and eastern English Channel largely disappeared after a crash in Herring stocks during the 1960s and 70s. A similar decline occurred around the Shetland Islands following the overfishing of sandeels in the 1980s, although both sandeels and Harbour Porpoises made a strong recovery in the 1990s. In some regions Harbour Porpoises appear resident whilst in other places they occur only seasonally. Numbers between Shetland and Yorkshire in the northern North Sea appear to peak in late summer, whereas sightings in the southern North Sea off Holland and East Anglia increase during the winter months.

Viewing hotspots

Easily seen from many headlands, particularly in the north and west of Great Britain. Good land-based viewing locations include Porthgwarra (Cornwall), Strumble Head (Pembrokeshire), Flamborough Head (Yorkshire), and Sumburgh Head (Shetland). Nearly all of Britain's whale and dolphin watching boats are located in areas frequented by Harbour Porpoises.

Centrally placed, short, triangular dorsal fin

Uniform grey back

Lacks a prominent beak

COMMON
BOTTLENOSE DOLPHIN
Tursiops Truncatus

Key identification features

This large, robust dolphin is one of the most familiar of all cetaceans, largely due to its playful acrobatic nature, popularity with the media, widespread use in aquaria and global distribution in coastal waters. Distinguished by its uniform grey colouration extending as far as the white belly, and the short, 'bottle-shaped' beak.

Behaviour

Common Bottlenose Dolphins are very active and curious animals and are capable of travelling at great speed. They regularly ride in the bow-wave and wake of passing vessels and often perform amazing acrobatics. Feeding occurs during the day and at night, hunting a variety of fish, squid and invertebrates so diverse that it would almost be easier to describe the prey that Common Bottlenose Dolphins don't eat rather than the prey that they do! Most commonly seen in pods of around 10 individuals, group sizes range between one and 40.

Distribution and habitat

A cosmopolitan species that occurs worldwide in temperate and tropical seas. Two distinct 'types' of Common Bottlenose Dolphin are generally recognised, although it is not possible to tell them apart at sea. The 'nearshore type' can be found in bays, lagoons and estuaries, whereas the 'offshore type' ranges widely away from the coast in shelf waters and deeper waters beyond the continental shelf. Common Bottlenose Dolphins are locally common in inshore waters throughout Europe as far north as Scotland.

In Great Britain this species is largely restricted to five regions where semi-resident populations persist. The most famous and well-studied groups of dolphins have home ranges centred in the Moray Firth, Scotland, and Cardigan Bay, Wales. Since 1991, Common Bottlenose Dolphins have also returned to South West England, with over 50 individuals known to roam throughout Cornwall, Devon and Dorset. Research suggests that these animals may form a roaming part of the Cardigan Bay population. Other discrete populations exist around the Western Isles of Scotland and around the Channel Islands.

Viewing hotspots

The population in the Moray Firth, which is the most northerly resident population in the world, is estimated at 130 animals, whilst around 200 animals frequent Cardigan Bay. These are amongst the most accessible places in Europe for dolphin watching, with numerous excellent coastal viewpoints as well as a selection of boat operators.

Photography: full page and left inset © AlexWilson / WildPics.org, right inset © Pete MacDonald

Short, but prominent, beak

Tall, centrally placed dorsal fin

Plain grey back with paler belly

RISSO'S DOLPHIN
Grampus griseus

Key identification features

The distinctive shape and colour of the Risso's Dolphin means that it is easily identified given good views. A large dolphin with a tall, curved dorsal fin, bulbous head and short beak. Pale grey to white in colour, Risso's Dolphins are unique amongst dolphins in having extensive body scarring.

Behaviour

When not feeding on a variety of fish, squid and Cuttlefish, Risso's Dolphins spend much of their time engaged in slow travel or resting at the surface. They are highly inquisitive animals and often breach, spy-hop and tail slap. Risso's Dolphins also sometimes exhibit aggressive behaviour towards each other, including flipper-slapping, striking each other with their tail flukes and dorsal fins and even striking full body blows. This explains why these dolphins are so heavily scarred. Being highly social, they frequently associate with other cetaceans, particularly Long-finned Pilot Whales, Sperm Whales, Short-beaked Common Dolphins and Common Bottlenose Dolphins. Group size ranges from one to 40 with an average of seven.

Distribution and habitat

Risso's Dolphins have a worldwide distribution in tropical to warm temperate waters where water temperature remains above 7.5ºC. In Europe this species is generally considered to favour deep offshore waters, although it is known to be resident in some shallow coastal zones towards the northern limit of its regular range to the west of Great Britain. Here, it is widely distributed throughout the Western Approaches to the English Channel, Irish Sea, and the Western and Northern Isles of Scotland. Photo-identification work in Scotland has confirmed that some individuals are present year-round, although sightings throughout Great Britain peak between May and September.

Viewing hotspots

Most regularly observed in the waters to the east of the Isle of Lewis, Western Isles. Tiumpan Head is a particularly good headland for land-based watching. Also irregularly encountered during offshore boat tours from West Wales.

Photography: full page and left inset
© Graeme Cresswell / breathtakingwhales.com,
right inset © hughharrop.com

Species Guide

Ghostly pale, heavily scarred body

Blunt head lacking a distinctive beak

Tall, pointed, centrally placed dorsal fin

SHORT-BEAKED
COMMON DOLPHIN
Delphinus delphis

Key identification features

This small, elegant dolphin has a slender beak and distinctive body pattern. The dark cape extends downwards below the dorsal fin to form a distinctive 'V'-shape. Behind the eye, the flanks are cream to yellow in colour, becoming grey on the tail stock.

Behaviour

A fast and energetic swimmer, readily attracted to the bow-wave and wake of passing ships. Often highly active, porpoising at high speed and creating a lot of spray. Short-beaked Common Dolphins regularly feed close to the surface and may be accompanied by seabirds in search of an opportunistic meal. The dolphins work together to herd fish into a tight ball trapped at the surface. The dolphins and seabirds then pick off individual fish. The majority of prey species in the Common Dolphin diet are pelagic fish. In deep waters, dolphins regularly dive to between 100m and 200m, typically catching Sardine and Sprat. However, during seasonal inshore movements to waters inside 100m depth, these dolphins select different prey, including Hake, Blue Whiting and Pollock. Associates with a number of other dolphin and whale species including Fin Whale, Sei Whale, Long-finned Pilot Whale and Striped Dolphin. Pod size varies from less than 10 to groups numbering in the hundreds.

Distribution and habitat

Widely distributed throughout the world's temperate and tropical seas. In Europe this species is considered to be the most abundant cetacean in offshore temperate waters, being widespread in both deep and shallow seas as far north as Scotland. In Great Britain it occurs throughout the Western Approaches to the English Channel, southern Irish Sea, and the Western Isles of Scotland, occasionally moving as far north as the Northern Isles. It is also occasionally sighted in the eastern English Channel, North Sea and northern Irish Sea. Dolphins present in deep water to the south of Great Britain in the Bay of Biscay during the summer months are thought to migrate inshore and over the shallow waters of the Western Approaches to the English Channel and the southern Irish Sea in late summer, remaining throughout the winter. Large numbers of stranded dolphins washed up along the coasts of Cornwall and Devon each winter show signs of entanglement in the nets of trawler fisheries operating offshore.

Viewing hotspots

The ferry from Penzance to the Isles of Scilly (Cornwall) can be excellent for sightings of this species in late summer and autumn. Boat trips offshore from West Wales also regularly encounter Common Dolphins during the summer months. Sightings are almost guaranteed year-round from the two ferries that cross the English Channel and the Bay of Biscay. They depart from Portsmouth and Plymouth.

Photography: full page and right inset © Dylan Walker / breathtakingwhales.com, left inset © Alex Wilson / WildPics.org

Relatively long beak

Striking yellow and grey criss-cross pattern on flank

Dark cape forms 'V'- shape below dorsal fin

Relatively small, slim body

ATLANTIC
WHITE-SIDED DOLPHIN
Lagenorhynchus acutus

Key identification features

A short-beaked, robust dolphin with a dark back and dorsal fin, grey flanks and a white belly. Distinguished by the sharply-defined white patch on the mid-flank, which extends along the tail stock as a thick yellow stripe.

Behaviour

Atlantic White-sided Dolphins are capable of acrobatic breaching and tail-slapping displays, but more usually they are seen moving rapidly through the water, revealing only the upper body as they surface. Although this species often occurs in small pods in inshore waters, larger schools of between 50 and 500 animals are commonly seen in deep water to the north-west of Scotland. Their social nature extends beyond members of their own species to include such cetaceans as Fin Whale, Humpback Whale, Long-finned Pilot Whale, Common Bottlenose Dolphin, White-beaked Dolphin and Short-beaked Common Dolphin. Unlike the closely related White-beaked Dolphin, Atlantic White-sided Dolphins generally favour fish over squid. Blue Whiting, Mackerel, Herring, Cod and Whiting are taken along with lesser quantities of squid and crustaceans.

Distribution and habitat

Confined to the cool temperate and sub-arctic waters of the North Atlantic. In Europe, Atlantic White-sided Dolphins are regularly recorded in deep waters to the west of Great Britain and Ireland and northwards to the Faroe Islands, Iceland and Norway. The British population is concentrated beyond 1,000m depth to the north-west of Scotland. However, between June and November the range expands to incorporate the shallow seas surrounding the Scottish mainland, even penetrating southwards into the northern North Sea.

Viewing hotspots

Fortune favours those who spot Atlantic White-sided Dolphins, which generally occur away from land and commercial whale watching areas. The best opportunities to see them are from ferries travelling to the Western and Northern Isles of Scotland, or across the northern North Sea.

Photography: full page and right inset © Dylan Walker / breathtakingwhales.com, left inset © hughharrop.com

Short beak

Upper back entirely black

Tall, pointed, centrally placed dorsal fin

Two-tone yellow and white patch on tail stock

Tricoloured black, grey and white face

WHITE-BEAKED DOLPHIN
Lagenorhynchus albirostris

Key identification features

At up to three metres in length, the White-beaked Dolphin appears stocky and robust as it surfaces to reveal a short beak and a tall dorsal fin. A strikingly black and white dolphin, the body is predominantly black with distinctive white areas on the beak, flank, behind the dorsal fin and on the belly. The name 'White-beaked' does not accurately describe its most diagnostic feature, as a few individuals have dark beaks.

Behaviour

A fast and powerful swimmer, which can be very acrobatic. Breaching sessions sometimes include as many as 20 continuous jumps at various angles, whilst tail-slapping is also frequently observed. White-beaked Dolphins are not shy and readily ride the bow-wave and wake of boats and ships. Rarely seen alone, they usually occur in small groups of between a few animals up to 50. Diet is predominantly composed of squid (in Newfoundland they are called "squid-hounds"), but they will also take Cod, Mackerel, Herring, Whiting, other fish and crustaceans, often hunting close to the sea floor.

Distribution and habitat

Confined to the cool temperate and sub-arctic seas of the North Atlantic, being widespread in Europe from Great Britain northwards to Iceland in shelf waters shallower than 200m. Present throughout Great Britain, White-beaked Dolphins occur most frequently in Scottish waters and in the North Sea. Sightings occur less frequently in the Irish Sea and the Western Approaches to the English Channel.

Remains rare in the English Channel and south into the Bay of Biscay, which represents the southern limit of this species' regular range. Sightings tend to peak during late summer when dolphins are more regularly encountered close to shore, although they are present in all seasons.

Viewing hotspots

Britain is one of the best places in the world to see White-beaked Dolphins, which are restricted to the cool waters of the North Atlantic. Sumburgh Head at the southern tip of mainland Shetland and the ferry route between Shetland and Fair Isle, where the North Sea meets the Atlantic Ocean, are particularly good places to look. The ferry crossing between Newcastle and Norway, which sails across the northern North Sea, is also gaining a reputation for regular sightings of this species.

Photography: full page © hughharrop.com, right inset © Dylan Walker / breathtakingwhales.com, left inset © Graeme Cresswell / breathtakingwhales.com

Large, centrally placed dorsal fin

Distinctive white flank and saddle patch

Short white beak visible from above

KILLER WHALE
Orcinus orca

Key identification features

Perhaps the most distinctive cetacean of all. The combination of the stocky, black body, white eye patch, grey saddle patch and prominent dorsal fin are unmistakable. Killer Whales travel in family groups, the members of which differ in the size and shape of their dorsal fins. The adult male is the most distinctive, with a broad, triangular dorsal fin reaching up to two metres in height. Females and immatures, which are significantly smaller in body length, have smaller, curved, dorsal fins.

Behaviour

The most powerful predator in the ocean. At up to nine tonnes in weight and 10m in length with a swimming speed of 23mph, the Killer Whale is capable of hunting fish, birds and marine mammals. Killer Whales live in family pods of between two and 30 individuals. The social nature of these animals means that they are very active at the surface, frequently breaching, spy-hopping, lobtailing, flipper-slapping and logging. Despite their inquisitiveness, Killer Whales rarely bow- or wake-ride passing vessels.

Distribution and habitat

With the exception of man, the Killer Whale is the most widespread mammal on earth. They occur in all oceans from the tropics to the edge of the pack ice in both Hemispheres, and are present in both inshore seas and deep, pelagic waters beyond the edge of the continental shelf. In Europe Killer Whales occur regularly around the coasts of northern Norway, Iceland, Great Britain and Ireland, and are present at lower densities in waters to the south, including the Iberian Peninsula and western Mediterranean. In Great Britain, Killer Whales are most abundant in Scottish waters, with less frequent sightings in the Irish Sea and the Western Approaches to the English Channel. They occur only rarely in the eastern English Channel and southern North Sea. Although Killer Whales are sighted throughout the year, the majority of records occur between May and October.

Viewing hotspots

Killer Whales roam over vast areas and are therefore highly unpredictable. The best place to see them in Great Britain is undoubtedly the Shetland Islands. Here, pods can be encountered irregularly throughout the year, but there is a significant increase in sightings during early summer, peaking in June. Photo-identification work by the *Shetland Sea Mammal Group* has established that stable groups of between two and 12 animals return to the islands year after year. These groups appear to be transient and rarely stay more than a few hours in one place. The large numbers of Common and Atlantic Grey Seals present at haul-out sites throughout the islands are believed to be the main draw for the whales, with up to four seals taken during a single attack. Although Killer Whales do not lunge for seals that are hauled out on the rocks, they often travel spectacularly close to the coast whilst hunting, offering whale watchers unparalleled viewing opportunities from land.

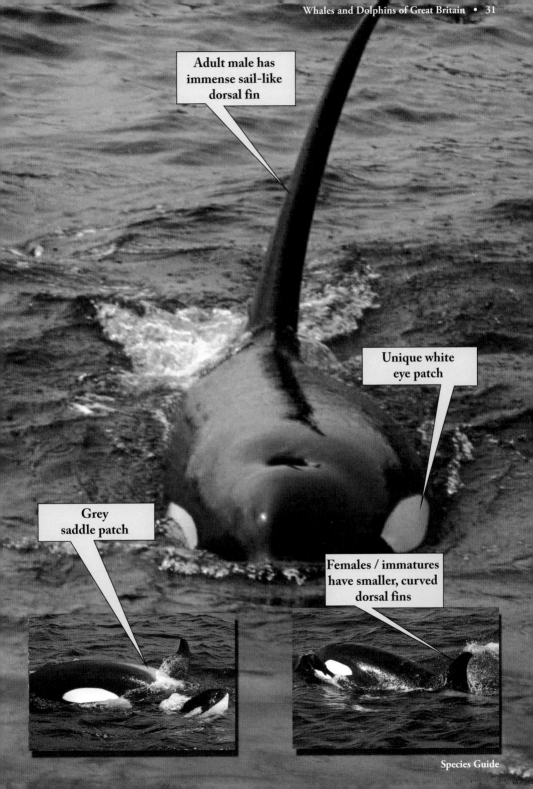

Adult male has immense sail-like dorsal fin

Unique white eye patch

Grey saddle patch

Females / immatures have smaller, curved dorsal fins

LONG-FINNED
PILOT WHALE
Globicephala melas

Key identification features

At 3.5-6.5m long, the Long-finned Pilot
Whale is easily identified by its shiny black
colouration, bulbous, rounded head and robust
body, with a dorsal fin set well forward on the
back. Generally occurring in family groups, the
dorsal fin shape varies with age and sex, with
the larger, broader dorsal fins belonging to
mature males.

Behaviour

The complex social lives and extensive
behavioural repertoire of the Long-finned Pilot
Whale make it one of the most interesting of
the cetaceans to observe at sea. These social
animals are usually seen in family groups,
resting or moving leisurely at the surface. They
are inquisitive, often approaching close to boats
before engaging in tail-slapping, flipper-
slapping and spy-hopping, although they rarely
breach or bow-ride. Associations with other
cetaceans are common, particularly with
Atlantic White-sided Dolphins but also with
Short-beaked Common Dolphins and
Common Bottlenose Dolphins. Typical group
size varies between one and 100.

Long-finned Pilot Whales hunt migrating
squid, Cuttlefish, Cod, Mackerel and a variety
of other fish, the unpredictable movements of
which appear to largely determine the
distribution of the whales. A large male Long-
finned Pilot whale has been estimated to
require nearly 250,000 squid (45 metric tons)
per year. In turn, Long-finned Pilot Whales are
still hunted to the north of Great Britain in the
Faroe Islands. This hunt operates in all months
and may take as many as several thousand Pilot
Whales and several dolphin species each year.

Distribution and habitat

Present throughout the sub-polar to warm
temperate waters of the world's oceans,
occurring both in deep pelagic waters and, less
frequently, in shallow shelf waters close to land.
Considered to be common and widespread in
Europe, occurring widely from Iceland and
Norway south to the Iberian Peninsula and the
Mediterranean Sea.

In Great Britain the Long-finned Pilot Whale
is abundant and widespread throughout the
deep waters to the north and west of Scotland.
Seasonal movements into coastal waters occur
mainly in two regions: around northern
Scotland between June and September, and in
the Western Approaches to the English
Channel in mid-winter. Even in these areas,
however, sightings are infrequent and fluctuate
annually and seasonally. The occasional
appearance of groups of Long-finned Pilot
Whales in the Western Approaches to the
English Channel during the summer months
has been linked to Cuttlefish migrations.

Viewing hotspots

Although unpredictable, Long-finned Pilot
Whales are sporadically sighted by ferry
passengers travelling in the western English
Channel en-route between Portsmouth and
Bilbao, or between Plymouth and Santander.

Broad-based, swept-back dorsal fin positioned two-fifths along the back

Black body glistens in sunshine

Blunt head lacks a prominent beak

Grey saddle patch (not visible here), usually visible

RARER SPECIES
Sperm, Fin, Sei and Humpback Whale

Key identification features

The **Sperm Whale** is the largest toothed cetacean and, at up to 18m long, is most likely to be mistaken for a baleen whale. **Sperm Whales** are characterised by a bulky body, large squarish head, and a dorsal hump positioned two-thirds of the way along the back. The blow is unique, as it is emitted from a single blowhole positioned to the left of the top of the head, producing a blow that is angled forward at a 45° angle when the whale exhales.

Three large baleen whales are seen occasionally in British waters. In increasing order of adult body length, they are: **Humpback Whale** (11-15m), **Sei Whale** (12-16m) and **Fin Whale** (18-26m). All are large enough to exhibit highly visible blows. Along with the much smaller Northern Minke Whale, the **Sei** and **Fin Whale** have been compared to Russian dolls as they are very similar in shape and colour but differ in size. All have dorsal fins set two-thirds of the way along the back, but the larger the species, the smaller the dorsal fin and the further along the back it appears. By observing the size and shape of the blow and dorsal fin, and the position of the fin in relation to the blowholes, it is therefore possible to tell the three species apart. The **Humpback Whale** is easier to identify. It has a tall, vertical blow that generally appears more bushy than that of the **Fin** and **Sei Whale**. However, it is best distinguished by the stubby 'humped' dorsal fin and variable white on the underside of the tail flukes, which becomes visible when the flukes are raised high before a deep dive. The pectoral flippers,

Humpback Whale

Relatively small dorsal fin positioned towards the tail

Tall bushy blow

'V' - shaped tail flukes have ragged edges. Undersides show variable amounts of white which are often lifted into the air, are exceptionally long at around one-third the length of the body.

Behaviour

Most sightings of **Fin** and **Sei Whales** in Britain involve lone animals on the move. Whilst travelling, both species surface regularly, emit vertical, highly visible blows and resist raising their tail flukes into the air prior to a deep dive. **Sperm Whales** occur alone or in small groups. The angled blow is bushy, the back lacks a dorsal fin and the tail flukes are usually raised prior to a deep dive. Of all the large whales, the **Humpback Whale** appears to be the most at home in shallow water, occasionally remaining in the same area for days or weeks in order to feed on Herring, sandeel or other schooling fish. Depending on the prey type and abundance, **Humpbacks** can work alone or in groups, displaying a range of hunting methods, many of which involve spectacular surface manoeuvres. Breaching, lobtailing and flipper-slapping may help in stunning or confusing prey, which may then be herded by trapping them inside walls of bubbles released through the blowholes in a technique called bubble netting.

Distribution and habitat

All four species of large whale occur mostly in deep offshore waters to the north, south and west of Britain. However, because they are highly migratory, they sometimes stray into the shallow waters surrounding our islands. **Fin**, **Sei** and **Humpback Whales** are also known to seek out shallow waters when in search of large concentrations of schooling prey species. By contrast, the **Sperm Whale** prefers very deep water, where it searches the murky depths for squid and a range of sharks, rays, bony fish and octopuses. Sightings of this species often involve groups or individuals near bays, estuaries or river mouths. Many of these animals appear lost and later strand on a nearby beach. The reasons for these strandings remain open to speculation.

Sei Whale

Fin Whale

Sperm Whale

Photography: left page © Alex Wilson / WildPics.org , top © Dylan Walker / breathtakingwhales.com, middle and bottom © hughharrop.com

Species Guide

RARER SPECIES
Cuvier's Beaked Whale, Sowerby's Beaked Whale, Northern Bottlenose Whale and Striped Dolphin

Key identification features

Three species of beaked whale occur with some regularity in British waters. All are generally shy, unobtrusive and prefer deep, offshore areas. Encounters with them are therefore rare. The largest of the three, at up to nine metres in length, is the **Northern Bottlenose Whale**. At the surface, it is very similar in appearance to a Minke Whale, having a curved dorsal fin situated two-thirds along the back and appearing uniform grey to brown in colouration. The large, bulbous head and protruding beak must be noted in order to make a positive identification. The head often becomes paler with age.

At up to seven metres in length, the **Cuvier's Beaked Whale** also has a small, curved dorsal fin placed well back on the body, and appears grey or brown. Again, head shape is diagnostic, with a gently sloping forehead that leads to a short but distinct beak. Pale areas often develop on the head and back of mature animals, the males of which also develop two protruding teeth at the tip of the lower jaw. Like the tusks of elephants, these teeth are used as weapons for fights between males, resulting in highly visible scarring on many individuals.

Sowerby's Beaked Whale has a similar body shape and colour to **Cuvier's Beaked Whale** and **Northern Bottlenose Whale,** but with an adult length of just under five metres it could also be mistaken for a dolphin. However, the position of the dorsal fin towards the tail and

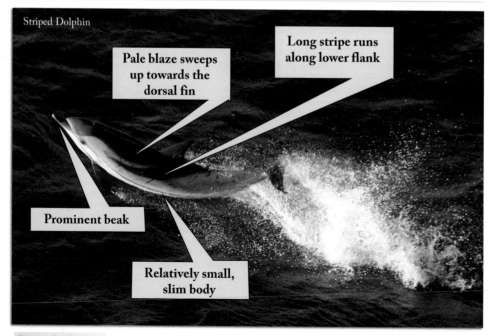

Striped Dolphin

Pale blaze sweeps up towards the dorsal fin

Long stripe runs along lower flank

Prominent beak

Relatively small, slim body

the exceptionally long beak distinguish **Sowerby's Beaked Whale** from all other cetaceans. In mature males, two flattened teeth protrude mid-way along the lower jaw, but this feature is almost impossible to observe at sea.

The **Striped Dolphin** is very similar to the Short-beaked Common Dolphin in size and shape, but is easily recognised by its distinctive markings. The grey body is strikingly marked by a thin, dark stripe that runs along the lower flanks, and a pale blaze that sweeps up towards the dorsal fin, dissecting the darker cape.

Behaviour

All three beaked whales may be seen alone or in small groups, generally moving leisurely at the surface. Spy-hopping, breaching and lobtailing are occasionally observed. Striped Dolphins generally occur in large, fast-moving groups of between 10 and 200 animals, often tail-slapping, breaching and travelling in arc-shaped leaps.

Distribution and habitat

The beaked whales spend their lives diving to great depths and for prolonged periods in search of deep-sea squid and fish. They therefore rarely venture close to shore. The most likely species to be seen in shallow water is the **Northern Bottlenose Whale**, with a handful of sightings every year. Following the discovery of the first **Sowerby's Beaked Whale** specimen on the Moray Firth coast by James Sowerby in 1800, more **Sowerby's Beaked Whales** have washed up along the shores of Great Britain than anywhere else in the world. The majority of these strandings have been spread throughout Scotland and along the North Sea coast, occurring throughout the year, with a peak in August. The handful of live sightings so far recorded have been in waters of depths beyond 500m to the north-west of Scotland along the Atlantic Frontier and the Faroe-Shetland Channel. Animals are present in these waters year-round with a marked increase in sightings

in August. Little is known of the status of **Cuvier's Beaked Whale**, which is commonly sighted to the south in the Bay of Biscay, but only known from a few strandings spread across Great Britain.

The **Striped Dolphin** lives in warm temperate waters, only ranging as far north as Britain sporadically. Most sightings are from the Western Approaches to the English Channel between July and December, although occasional observations and strandings occur as far north as the Shetland Islands.

Cuvier's Beaked Whale

Northern Bottlenose Whale

Sowerby's Beaked Whale

Photography: left page © hughharrop.com, right page © Dylan Walker / breathtakingwhales.com

WHERE TO GO WHALE AND DOLPHIN WATCHING

The following pages will dispel forever the myth that in order to have amazing encounters with whales and dolphins, you have to travel abroad. In the last few years, Great Britain has really begun to realise its potential as a world-class destination for watching these charismatic marine mammals. This chapter will illustrate, not only the incredible diversity of species to be seen, but also the many options that exist to go out and spot them, from gazing out to sea from one of our many headlands, to taking ferries, high-speed inflatable boats, yachts, ex-fishing trawlers, purpose-built whale watching vessels and even cruise ships. All are utilised for one simple purpose, to allow us a glimpse into the lives of the most inspiring animals in our seas – the cetaceans. So if you would like to see a wild dolphin, whale, or porpoise in Britain, simply continue from this page and find out how!

FLAMBOROUGH HEAD

Introduction: These 100m high cliffs project eastwards into the central North Sea, supporting one of England's premier seabird colonies and offering sweeping views.

Species and season: Although the sea here is considered to be poor for cetaceans, good numbers of Harbour Porpoises gather close to the cliffs between May and September, and Northern Minke Whales are sometimes present in late summer. White-beaked Dolphins are occasionally seen in winter, and rarities have included Atlantic White-sided Dolphin, Killer Whale, Sperm Whale and Fin Whale. Gannets, Kittiwakes and Fulmars breed on the cliffs at nearby Bempton RSPB Reserve, whilst large numbers of terns, skuas and shearwaters pass close by in late summer.

How to get there: Take the B1229 or B1255 to Flamborough Village then turn off on to the B1259. Park by the lighthouse and walk to a safe viewpoint for panoramic views.

Location: Flamborough Head, Yorkshire

Photography: left page, whale watchers on Caliach Point in north-west Mull © Alex Carlisle, *right page,* Flamborough Head © Toni Cross / WildPics.org

Land-based Listing

WEYBOURNE

Introduction: Harbour Porpoises are widespread close to shore along the north and east coasts of Norfolk but the low-lying nature of this stretch of coastline makes them difficult to view. Porpoises are regularly sighted by birdwatchers from the shore at Cley and Titchwell nature reserves. However, the elevated viewing provided from the cliffs at Weybourne make it the best place to watch this species along the Norfolk coast.

Weybourne may also be advantageous for cetacean watching because of the relative depth of the water close to shore. The steep pebble beach gives way to a small underwater canyon here, the tip of which reveals itself as marshy ground cutting 100m inland towards Weybourne village. Indeed, this is the only place in Norfolk considered to have been deep enough for submarines to have approached close to land during World War II.

Species and season: Harbour Porpoises are probably present year-round but are seen more regularly throughout the spring and summer months when weather conditions make this small cetacean easier to spot. Other cetaceans are very rare here but large whales have been reported on a few occasions. Small numbers of Common Bottlenose Dolphins have also been seen along the North Norfolk coast in recent summers, so this species may also occur occasionally.

How to get there: From Sheringham, follow the A149 coast road until you enter the village of Weybourne. Pass the church and turn right by the village shop. Follow the road down to the beach car park. Take the coastal path eastwards towards Sheringham, which rises up as a cliff. View northwards from the cliffs. Choose a calm day.

Facilities: Weybourne village has a pub, a hotel with a restaurant, and a village shop.

Location:
Weybourne, Norfolk

Photography:
Harbour Porpoise
© Alex Carlisle

Land-based Listing

THE COMPANY OF WHALES

Introducing the location: There are few locations in the world that offer such an extraordinary diversity of marine life as the Bay of Biscay. With *The Company of Whales* you will travel onboard the cruise-ferry *Pride of Bilbao*, through the rich, deep waters of the Bay of Biscay in search of whales, dolphins, seabirds and sharks.

Species: Fin, Minke, Cuvier's Beaked and Pilot Whales along with Harbour Porpoise, Short-beaked Common, Striped and Common Bottlenose Dolphins seen on most departures. Less frequently recorded species include Risso's Dolphin, Sowerby's Beaked Whale, Killer Whale, and Sperm Whale. True's Beaked Whale has been recorded on two occasions. Also a great opportunity to see Basking Shark and Yellow-fin Tuna. Seabirds include six species of shearwater (including Little Shearwater), four species of skua, Sabine's Gull, Storm & Leach's Petrels, and Grey Phalarope.

Trip details: A total of 25 trips per year, departing Portsmouth for three-night cruises. Exclusive access to viewing platform for *Company of Whales* guests. Maximum group size of 30 travellers.

Operating season: June to the end of September annually.

Price: From £235 per person for a three-night cruise.

Departure time and duration: Cruises depart Portsmouth at 21:15 on day one and return to Portsmouth at 17:15 on day four.

Departure location and how to get there: Portsmouth is linked by an excellent series of road and rail networks. Southampton airport is 30 miles from Portsmouth.

Naturalist guides: The team includes some of Britain's leading experts on marine mammals. All are hand-picked for their field experience and are superb all-rounders, with an understanding of all aspects of natural history.

Vessel details: *Pride of Bilbao*: 37,700 tonnes and 177 metres long. The only way to cross Biscay in comfort!

Photographic opportunities: Excellent. A 300mm or larger lens in recommended for best results.

Conservation / Research: *The Company of Whales* is the primary collector of research data in the Bay of Biscay, with around 25 surveys taking place between April and October every year. This data has contributed significantly to our understanding of the distribution and relative abundance of marine life. Also financially support the work of numerous conservation charities, many working full-time to protect the marine environment.

Location:
Portsmouth – Bilbao, sailing through the English Channel and Bay of Biscay

Website: www. companyofwhales.co.uk

Telephone: 01950 422483

Fax: 01950 422430

E-mail: info@ companyofwhales.co.uk

Address:
Longhill, Maywick, Shetland, UK, ZE2 9JF

Boat-based Listing

ST. CATHERINE'S BREAKWATER

Introduction: This long breakwater juts out from the north east corner of the island of Jersey to offer an unusual viewing promontory.

Species and season: Several pods of Common Bottlenose Dolphins from Jersey's resident population pass very close to St. Catherine's Breakwater daily on their way to important feeding grounds in nearby Fliquet Bay and Bouley Bay. Frequently observed behaviours include travelling, playing, feeding, speed swimming and associating with boats. Pod sizes range from two to 30 with an average of 10. Movements vary with the tide and season. Try asking local fishermen for advice on recent sightings and the best time of day to watch.

How to get there: Take the A4 east to Gorey and follow the signs to St Catherine's. Park and walk to the end of the breakwater.

Facilities: Café, parking and toilets.

Location:
St. Catherine's
Breakwater, Jersey

Contact:
Jersey Tourism,
Liberation Square,
St Helier, Jersey,
JE1 1BB

Telephone:
01534 44880

Photography:
Common Bottlenose
Dolphins
© Steve Hartley

Land-based Listing

DURLSTON COUNTRY PARK

Introduction: Situated on Durlston Head, which forms part of the Isle of Purbeck to the south of Bournemouth, Dorset. The Durlston Marine Project, which is based at the Country Park, monitors the local Common Bottlenose Dolphins by recording sightings and listening to a hydrophone placed on the sea floor. The hydrophone is linked to a speaker so that it is occasionally possible to hear vocalisations live.

Species and season: Common Bottlenose Dolphins are present sporadically off the coast throughout the year.

How to get there: From Bournemouth or Poole, take the A351 through Wareham and south to Swanage. Follow the minor coast road to the south of Swanage, which terminates at Durlston Country Park Visitor Centre.

Facilities: The Visitor Centre includes exhibits on sounds from under the sea and shows live video pictures of the nearby seabird colonies. Other facilities include a shop, toilets and a viewing hide. The centre is open 10:00 – 17:00 from Easter to October, and 10:30 – 16:00 on weekends and school holidays only between November and March. There are also picnic tables outside.

Location:
Durlston Country Park, Dorset

Contact:
Durlston Country Park, Lighthouse Road, Swanage, Dorset, BH19 2JL

Telephone:
01929 424443

E-mail:
info@durlston.co.uk

Website: www. durlston.co.uk/marine

Photography:
Common Bottlenose Dolphin © Alex Wilson / WildPics.org

Land-based Listing

ULTIMATE PELAGICS

Introducing the location: The nutrient rich area of the Bay of Biscay has produced sightings of over 20 different species of whales, dolphins and porpoises. Over 2,500 cetaceans were recorded on the four day trip last year, perhaps explaining why the Bay of Biscay is such a hotspot for whale and dolphin watching.

The second area travelled to is Ireland, named by the Irish government in 1991 as the first whale and dolphin sanctuary of its kind in Europe. To date 24 species of cetacean have been recorded, 11 of which are thought to breed, while a further five migrate annually through Irish waters.

Species: Fin Whale, Long-finned Pilot Whale, Northern Minke Whale, Cuvier's Beaked Whale, Northern Bottlenose Whale, Sei Whale, False Killer Whale, Killer Whale, Blue Whale, and Sperm Whale. Short-beaked Common, Common Bottlenose, Striped and Risso's Dolphin, Harbour Porpoise, Basking Shark and Ocean Sunfish.

Trip details: This fully dedicated sea watching cruise departs from Falmouth in Cornwall or Plymouth in Devon, onboard a luxury cruise liner to search these nutrient rich areas for marine life.

Operating season: Late July and August.

Price: Prices start from £350 per person and include accommodation onboard and all meals.

Departure time and duration: Early evening for this multi-day cruise.

Location:
Plymouth, Devon

Name of operator:
Ultimate Pelagics Ltd

Website: www. ultimatepelagics.com

Telephone:
01202 606356

Fax:
01202 606064

E-mail: info@ ultimatepelagics.com

Address:
4a Plymouth Road, Plymouth, Devon, PL7 4JR

Departure location and how to get there: Contact *Ultimate Pelagics*, as the departure location may be either Falmouth in Cornwall, or Plymouth.

Naturalist guides: Thirty guides onboard, including a team from the onboard research charity *Biscay Dolphin Research Programme*, with a full PA system announcing all sightings.

Vessel details: The *MV Athena* is a fully stabilised and air-conditioned cruise ship providing a luxury platform to view the wildlife on offer.

Photographic opportunities: These trips provide an excellent and stable platform for photography. The weather in August is usually very good for watching whales and dolphins.

Conservation / Research: Ultimate Pelagics works closely with the Biscay Dolphin Research Programme to promote and enhance conservation of marine life in a manner consistent with sustainable development.

FOWEY MARINE ADVENTURES

Introducing the location: Fowey Harbour is a natural deep-water estuary situated on the south coast in an area known as the Cornish Riviera. The coastline around Fowey is a designated *Area of Outstanding Natural Beauty (AONB)*.

Species: Short-beaked Common Dolphin, Common Bottlenose Dolphin, Long-finned Pilot Whale, Fin Whale, and Risso's Dolphin.

Trip details: The trips are onboard a purpose-built passenger vessel able to carry up to 12 passengers and two crew. Trips explore both the coastline and the surrounding waters.

Operating season: All year.

Price: Adults £20, children (under 14 years) £15.

Departure time and duration: 10:00, 12:30 and 15:00. Scheduled trips last one and a half hours. Longer trips can be arranged.

Departure location and how to get there: Fowey is reached from the A390. From St. Austell turn right at the roundabout signposted 'Par' and 'Fowey'. From Lostwithiel turn left after one mile signposted 'Fowey' and follow the road to the roundabout at four turnings, on the outskirts of Fowey. The vessel departs from the Town Quay.

Vessel details: The *Kernow Explorer* is a 10m long purpose-built passenger vessel, MCA licensed to carry 12 passengers plus two crew up to 20 miles offshore.

Photographic opportunities: Due to the open layout of the boat, passengers are provided with excellent views and photographic opportunities.

Conservation / Research: The crew is *WiSe* (*Wildlife Safe operator accredited*) and follows all codes of conduct designed to protect the marine environment. All sightings are recorded and all photographs are passed on to the *Cornwall Wildlife Trust*, of which *Fowey Marine Adventures* are corporate members.

Location:
Fowey, Cornwall

Name of operator:
Fowey Marine Adventures

Website: www. fma.fowey.com

Telephone:
01726 832300

E-mail:
fma@fowey.com

Address:
35 Fore Street, Fowey, Cornwall, PL23 1BY

Boat-based Listing

LIZARD POINT

Introduction: Approximately seven miles south of Helston, Lizard Point is the most southerly headland on the mainland coast of England. An Area of Outstanding Natural Beauty, it is comprised of heathland, rare serpentine rocky outcrops and dramatic cliffs overlooking the sea.

Species and season: In summer, Lizard Point is one of the best places in Europe to view Basking Sharks from shore, with over 50 recorded on some calm days. Cetaceans are also regularly sighted, especially Harbour Porpoise and Short-beaked Common Dolphin. Common Bottlenose Dolphin, Killer Whale, Northern Minke Whale and Risso's Dolphin are seen occasionally.

How to get there: By car from Helston, take the A3083 south to Church Cove or Lizard town. Lizard Point lies half a mile from Church Cove and is well signposted.

Facilities: There is a *National Trust* car park and toilet at Lizard Point. Alternatively, there is free parking in Lizard town, from where a footpath leads to Lizard Point, where there is a café.

Contact:
Lizard Heritage
Tourist Association.
Telephone:
01326 281079

Photography:
© Dan Jarvis

Land-based Listing

MARINE DISCOVERY PENZANCE

Introducing the location: The far west of Cornwall is home to an abundance of marine mammals amidst beautiful surroundings. Penzance is a bustling town, with a good variety of restaurants, pubs and places to stay.

Species: Grey Seal, Harbour Porpoise, Common Bottlenose and Short-beaked Common Dolphins, Basking Shark, Ocean Sunfish (summer), and a variety of seabirds and other fish. Rarer encounters include Risso's Dolphin, Minke Whale, Long-finned Pilot Whale, and Fin Whale.

Trip details: A variety of trips to suit different ages and budgets. These include the one hour Bay Discovery, the two hour Marine Discovery and the two and a half hour Ocean Discovery (see website for details).

Operating season: March to October. Winter trips possible.

Price: £12 to £36 depending on the trip length.

Departure time and duration: Trips run daily, lasting up to two and a half hours. Departure times vary.

Departure location and how to get there: From Penzance Harbour: the South Pier (low tide) or the Albert Pier (high tide). Marine Discovery's office is located on the Albert Pier. Penzance Harbour is situated next to the bus and railway station and the main town car park.

Naturalist guides: The skipper holds a BSc in Marine Ecology and Oceanography. Skipper and crew have extensive knowledge of the wildlife and heritage of the area and are qualified teachers.

Vessel details: Trips are run on the 8-metre jet RIB *Shearwater*. The vessel is fully licensed by the MCA and can take 12 passengers.

Photographic opportunities: Plenty! When the light is right, the colours of West Cornwall are simply stunning. Passengers are encouraged to send in their wildlife photographs for identification purposes.

Conservation / Research: A founder member of the *Marine Conservation Society's* Corporate Partnership scheme, and has also been chosen by the *Marine Connection* to run their marine wildlife watching trips in the South West. Has also carried out research trips with various organisations including universities and conservation organisations, and has been used several times by the *BBC Natural History Unit*. Wildlife sightings are recorded and submitted to various organisations for research.

Location:
Penzance, Cornwall

Name of operator:
Marine Discovery, Penzance

Website: www. marinediscovery.co.uk

Telephone: 01736 874907

Mobile: 07749 277110

E-mail: info@ marinediscovery.co.uk

Address: 5 Gulval Cross, Gulval, Penzance, Cornwall, TR18 3BN

Boat-based Listing

ELEMENTAL TOURS

Introducing the location: Bringing together all the elements that make West Cornwall such a special corner of the British Isles, *Elemental Tours* aims to raise awareness of the wealth of natural, historic and cultural heritage in West Cornwall, and create a real and lasting experience of this unique and magical place.

Species: Depending on the time of the year, it is possible to encounter a range of cetacean species including Harbour Porpoise, Common Bottlenose Dolphin, Risso's Dolphin, Short-beaked Common Dolphin, Northern Minke Whale, Long-finned Pilot Whale, and the occasional Killer Whale. Even Fin Whale, the second largest animal on the planet, has been sighted. Atlantic Grey Seals are resident all year round, whilst Basking Sharks and Ocean Sunfish are also regular in spring and summer.

Trip details: Operating all year round, Penzance and Cornwall's first wildlife watching company offers exciting, fun-packed, expertly guided boat trips, walks and overland eco-tours. Trips depart from Penzance harbour and travel along the magnificent coastline around either Land's End or the Lizard Peninsula, and out into the Atlantic Ocean, passing many well known landmarks, including St. Michael's Mount and the Minack Theatre.

Operating season:
All year weather permitting.

Price: Two hour Atlantic Adventure trip: adult £30, child (5-15 years old) £20. Three hour Ocean Safari trip: adult £35, child £30.

Departure time and duration: Atlantic Adventure trips last for two hours and cover at least 25 miles during that time. Longer three or four hour Ocean Safaris Penzance trips are occasionally run if certain species are around, or if a charter group request it.

Departure location and how to get there: Albert pier, Penzance harbour. Next to mainline train and bus stations, and a large car park.

Naturalist guides: The skipper began working on pleasure boats as crew and guide in Cornwall over thirty years ago, and the other guides have a long, close association with wildlife organisations in the area.

Vessel details: *Ocean Ranger* is a nine metre long RIB, licensed for 12 passengers and two crew. The outboard motors are low emission, and top quality life jackets are provided.

Photographic opportunities: Very good. Indeed, clients are encouraged to participate in photo-identification projects.

Conservation / Research: *Elemental Tours* have a strong commitment to ethical tourism and conservation. They work closely with *Cornwall Wildlife Trust*, *Marine Conservation Society*, and the *Shark Trust*. They also raise funds for wildlife charities. Staff are trained members of the local cetacean strandings network, and are also *British Divers Marine Life Rescue* medics.

Location:
Penzance, West Cornwall

Name of operator:
Elemental Tours Ltd

Website: www. elementaltours.co.uk

Telephone:
01736 811200 /
07971 540280

E-mail:
elementaltours@ blue-earth.co.uk

Address:
Tregonebris Cottage,
Tregonebris, Sancreed, Cornwall,
TR20 8RQ

SILVER DOLPHIN CENTRE

Introducing the location:
Located in beautiful Mounts Bay,
Penzance, and the ideal location for
cetacean watching.

Species: Common Bottlenose
Dolphin, Short-beaked Common
Dolphin, Northern Minke Whale and
Harbour Porpoise are sighted year
round. White-beaked Dolphin may be
seen in August, whilst Fin Whale,
Long-finned Pilot Whale, Risso's
Dolphin and Striped Dolphin
occur occasionally.

Trip details: Trips head west towards
Land's End or east towards the Lizard.

Operating season: All year, trips are
weather dependent.

Price: RIB £35 for a 2 hour trip.
Hard boat £20 for a 2 hour trip.

Departure time and duration:
Trips depart at 10:00 and 13:00,
lasting for two hours. Longer trips can
be arranged.

**Departure location and how to
get there:** Trips begin at the Centre
with a briefing on the work of the
Silver Dolphin Centre and the local
marine life. The Centre is located on
Penzance harbour front and has its
own private car parking.
It is within easy
walking distance of trains and buses.

Naturalist guides: A member of
staff who is experienced in cetacean
watching accompanies all trips.

Vessel details: See 'Price' section.

Photographic opportunities:
Excellent photographic opportunities.
Visitors are encouraged to add their
pictures to the Centre's photographic
identification database.

Conservation / Research: All trips
are based on research work being carried
out at the Centre. Data on all sightings
and strandings are recorded in order to
build a picture of the distribution of
cetaceans around the Cornish coast.
Silver Dolphin Centre staff are *WiSe*
(*Wildlife Safe operator accredited*) and are
members of the Police and *DEFRA
Partnership Against Wildlife Crime* (*PAW*).
Boat trips follow a code of conduct and
ensure that there is no harassment of the
animals. *Cornish Marine Life Rescue*, a
voluntary group run by the Centre, is
responsible for rescuing stranded
cetaceans and recording evidence of
entanglement in fishing nets. *The Silver
Dolphin Centre* also runs workshops
and longer courses for
schools, colleges and
groups from
the UK and
from
abroad.

Location:
Penzance, Cornwall

Name of operator:
Silver Dolphin
Centre

Website: www.
silverdolphinmarine
conservationanddivi
ng.co.uk

Telephone:
01736 364860

E-mail:
conservation@
silverdolphin.freeserve.
co.uk

Address:
Trinity House,
Wharf Road,
Penzance, Cornwall,
TR18 4BN

Boat-based Listing

MINACK THEATRE

Introduction: The Minack Theatre is an open-air theatre built into the cliffside and facing the ocean near Land's End. Built in the 1920s, the theatre affords such stunning views over the sea that the actors sometimes find themselves with the dubious privilege of competing for attention with leaping dolphins in the bay below!

Species and season: Short-beaked Common Dolphin, Common Bottlenose Dolphin, Risso's Dolphin, and Harbour Porpoise are all seen regularly by dedicated observers, as are Basking Sharks and seals.

How to get there: Follow the A30 south west past Penzance, then turn slightly left on to the B3283. Follow this road as it becomes the B3315 until you arrive at Porthcurno. At the seaward end of the valley go up the winding hill and the theatre entrance is on the left. Parking in the large car park is free.

Facilities: The theatre and surrounding gardens are open every day to paying visitors from 9:30 to 17:30. There is a coffee shop and gift shop on site.

Contact:
The Minack
Theatre,
Porthcurno,
Penzance, Cornwall,
TR19 6JU

Telephone:
01736 810181 or
810471

E-mail:
info@minack.com

Website:
www.minack.com

Photography:
© Alex Wilson /
WildPics.org

Land-based Listing

GWENNAP HEAD

Introduction: Situated at the far south-west of Cornwall and facing out across the Atlantic Ocean, the coastal path along the top of the granite cliffs of Gwennap Head offers spectacular views.

Species and season: This is one of the best seawatching sites in England, famous for inshore movements of shearwaters, petrels and skuas during periods of prolonged onshore winds. On calmer days, look out for Harbour Porpoise and Northern Minke Whale. Short-beaked Common Dolphin is also present in these waters, along with occasional Risso's Dolphin and Killer Whale. Seals are present in the cove at nearby Porthgwarra and Basking Sharks are regularly sighted close inshore.

How to get there: About 30 minutes drive from Penzance. Follow the A30 around the Penzance bypass. Turn left on to the B3315 via Newlyn, following the road for six miles before turning left on to a minor road signposted for Porthgwarra. Park in the village and walk to the headland.

Facilities: Porthgwarra is a small hamlet with a sandy cove. There is a small shop/cafe open during the summer season selling food and drink. There are public toilets and a public telephone.

Location:
Gwennap Head,
Cornwall

Website:
www. sennen-
cove.com/pg.htm

Photography:
© Dan Jarvis

Land-based Listing

CAPE CORNWALL

Introduction: The only place in England to be named a 'cape', this headland, guarded by an old minestack, provides for a beautiful and unspoilt landscape alive with wildflowers. Views out to the Western Approaches to the English Channel encompass The Brisons, an underwater reef that has caused many ships to founder. This dramatic stretch of coastline is situated five miles north of Land's End and one mile to the west of St. Just.

Species and season: Although views are sometimes distant, those with good binoculars or a telescope can enjoy excellent land-based marine mammal and seabird watching. This site is probably the best place in England to see Risso's Dolphins, which are recorded sporadically throughout the

year. More obvious are the Common and Atlantic Grey Seals basking on the rocks, whilst Harbour Porpoises feed on the rising tide. Other summer sightings include Short-beaked Common Dolphin, Common Bottlenose Dolphin, Northern Minke Whale, Killer Whale and Basking Shark, whilst Long-finned Pilot Whale and Fin Whale put in occasional appearances during the winter months.

How to get there: From Penzance, take the A3071 to St. Just. In St. Just, take a minor road to Cape Cornwall and park where the road terminates. A coastal path winds down to the Cape.

Facilities: There are many facilities in the nearby town of St Just.

Location:
Cape Cornwall,
Cornwall

Contact:
St. Just Tourist
Information Centre,
The Library, Market
Street, St Just,
Penzance, Cornwall,
TR19 7HX

Telephone:
01736 788669

Fax:
01736 788586

E-mail:
stjust.library@
cornwall.gov.uk

Website: www.
go-cornwall.com

Photography
© Alex Wilson /
WildPics.org

Land-based Listing

VOYAGES OF DISCOVERY

Introducing the location: Ramsey Island, famed for its wildlife, with one of the UK's largest Atlantic Grey Seal colonies, offering superb seal watching. Ramsey Sound holds a resident population of Harbour Porpoises. Offshore, nutrient-rich waters from the Atlantic produce a prolific ecosystem on the edge of the Celtic Deep, one of the few places in the Great Britain where cetaceans, seals and birdlife can be found in large numbers.

Species: Ramsey: Atlantic Grey Seal, Harbour Porpoise and Ocean Sunfish. Birds include Kittiwake, Guillemot, Razorbill, Chough and Peregrine Falcon. Offshore: Short-beaked Common and Risso's Dolphin, Minke, Fin, Sei, Long-finned Pilot and Killer Whales, Harbour Porpoise, Basking Shark, seals, Gannet, Puffin and several species of shearwater.

Trip details: A non-stop mixture of sensitive wildlife observation and exhilaration. On every voyage, a professional guide aims to provide an interactive tour, stopping at all points of interest to talk about the islands and make the most of the opportunities to photograph wildlife. A combination of experience and the use of purpose-built specialist vessels designed to navigate the intricate coastline and tides provide for breathtakingly close encounters.

Operating season: Open All Year. Ramsey voyages run from the end of March to the end of October, with limited winter sailings. Offshore voyages run from the end of May to the end of September.

Price: Ramsey voyages: adults £22, children (12 years and under) £12, toddlers (under four years) £5. Offshore: adults £50, children (8 –12 years) £25.

Departure time and duration: One hour Ramsey Island voyages departing hourly. Offshore Voyage departs every morning for two and a half hours to Grassholm Island, and then up to 20 miles offshore.

Departure location and how to get there: Booking Office is located in the centre of St Davids on the Cross Square, opposite Lloyds Bank. Voyages depart from St Justinians Lifeboat Station, two miles from St Davids.

Naturalist guides: Vessels operated by qualified skippers and crews including former RNLI Coxwain and present lifeboat crew members, marine biologists and conservationists, all highly experienced with a wealth of knowledge about the islands and the wildlife.

Vessel details: Fleet of purpose-built Rigid Hull Inflatable Boats. All are very stable, highly manoeuvrable, ideal wildlife watching platforms, providing for personalised interactive tours.

Photographic opportunities: Photographers delight due to the close proximity of rare species; rock ledges teeming with seabirds; awesome, spellbinding landscape of deep sea-caves, towering sea-cliffs and breathtaking rock-gorges.

Conservation / Research: Carbon neutral company, *WiSe* accredited, and a founder member of the *Pembrokeshire Marine Code*.

Location:
St Davids,
Pembrokeshire

Name of operator:
Voyages Of
Discovery

Website: www.
ramseyisland.co.uk

Telephone:
01437 721911

Freephone:
0800 854367

Fax:
01437 720092

E-mail: john@
ramseyisland.co.uk

Address:
1 High Street, St
Davids, SA62 6SA

Boat-based Listing

STRUMBLE HEAD

Introduction: At the tip of the Pencaer Peninsula, Strumble Head protrudes northwards into Cardigan Bay, offering excellent views of the southern Irish Sea. The best and most sheltered viewpoint is on the seaward side of a grey unmanned observation building originally built in the Second World War. To the left you will see the Strumble Head Lighthouse, which perches on top of a small islet called Ynysmeicl (St. Michael's Island).

Species and season: Famed as the best location in Wales to watch seabirds, Strumble Head is a popular place for birdwatchers, particularly during the autumn seabird migration season. At this time of year, strong south-westerly winds veering to the west or north-west can result in large numbers of many bird species passing by close to shore. On calm days, Strumble Head is an excellent place to view Harbour Porpoises, which feed amongst the tidal races between the headland and Strumble Bank. Other cetaceans are sighted very occasionally, including Common Bottlenose Dolphin and Risso's Dolphin. Atlantic Grey Seals are present year-round along this stretch of coast, with pups often visible during late autumn.

How to get there: From Fishguard, take the minor road north-west for approximately three miles until you reach Strumble Head.

Facilities: There are many facilities in the nearby town of Fishguard.

Location:
Strumble Head,
Pembrokeshire

Photography:
© Stephen Berry

Land-based Listing

A BAY TO REMEMBER

Introducing the location: Cardigan and Aberporth are in the southern part of Cardigan Bay on the west coast of Wales, located in a *Special Area of Conservation.*

Species: Regular sightings of Common Bottlenose Dolphin, Harbour Porpoise and Atlantic Grey Seal. Other species sighted occasionally include Basking Shark, Ocean Sunfish, Humpback Whale, Northern Minke Whale and Killer Whale.

Trip details: Bay Explorer tour is a 60 to 90 minute family favourite, exploring the caves around Cemaes Head (yes the boat will fit inside the caves!) and also circumnavigating Cardigan Island, where seals are seen virtually every day in the caves and on the rocks. The cruise then continues on up the coast to explore Mwnt and / or Aberporth, which are both popular feeding areas for the resident Common Bottlenose Dolphins.
 The Offshore Explorer tour is a two to two and a half hour specialist tour for the keen wildlife lover. It incorporates the Bay Explorer tour and, in addition, continues out to the less-explored and deeper offshore waters in search of other visiting cetaceans.

Operating season: Open all year but with limited winter sailings.

Price: Bay Explorer tour: adults £20, children £10. Offshore Explorer tour: adults £55, children £30.

Departure time and duration: Departure times are dependent on tide and weather conditions. Trips last from one to two and a half hours.

Departure location and how to get there: Depart from either Gwbert, which is just outside Cardigan, or Aberporth Beach. Visit the website for a detailed map.

Naturalist guides: All tours are fully guided by the crew and skippers, who are fully trained on the local wildlife and the coastline.

Vessel details: Purpose-built 10m RIB with the latest low emission outboard engines.

Photographic opportunities: Plenty.

Conservation / Research: *WiSe* (*Wildlife Safe operator accredited*), members of the *Pembrokeshire Marine Code* and adhere to the *Ceredigion commercial operators' code of conduct.* Also Green Dragon Level 2 and aiming to be Carbon Neutral by the end of 2007.

Location:
Cardigan, Ceredigion

Name of operator:
A Bay To Remember

Website: www. baytoremember.co.uk

Telephone:
01239 810482

Fax:
01239 800113

E-mail: tony@ baytoremember.co.uk

Address:
Saffron, Parcllyn, Cardigan, Ceredigion, SA43 2DR

Boat-based Listing

NEW QUAY BOAT TRIPS

Introducing the location: New Quay is a small picturesque village in the heart of Cardigan Bay, boasting a glorious sandy beach. The *Ceredigion Marine Heritage Coast* is recognised for its unspoilt coastline and wildlife.

Species: Common Bottlenose Dolphin, Atlantic Grey Seal, Harbour Porpoise and a variety of seabirds.

Trip details: One and two hour trips along the *Ceredigion Marine Heritage Coast*, visiting Seal Bay, Bird Rock, Cwmtydu, Ynys Lochtyn and a number of sea caves. The dolphins are wild and cannot be guaranteed on every trip. However, they are a regular and awe inspiring sight.

Operating Season: April – October.

Price: One hour tour: adults £6, children £3. Two hour tour: adults £12, children £6. Ten percent discount offered for groups of 10 people and over.

Location:
New Quay, Ceredigion

Name of operator:
New Quay Boat Trips

Website: www. newquayboattrips.co .uk

Telephone:
01545 560375 (evening), 01545 560800 (daytime)

Fax:
01545 560375

E-mail: nqboats@ ntlworld.com

Address:
The Moorings, Glanmore Terrace, New Quay, Ceredigion, SA45 9PS

Departure time and duration: Trips depart daily. One hour trips depart every hour from 11:00. Two hour trips depart every two hours from 11:30. Trip times depend on the tides so it is essential to ring in advance.

Departure location and how to get there: Boat trips leave from the main pier, New Quay, which is situated 26 miles south of Aberystwyth, and 35 miles west of Carmarthen, weather permitting.

Vessel details: Two vessels are in operation. *The Ermol 6* passenger vessel licensed to carry 67 passengers, and *The Ermol 5* passenger vessel licensed to carry 50 passengers. Both vessels are licensed by the *MCA* and the skippers are qualified boatmasters.

Photographic opportunities: Both boats are open-topped, allowing marvellous photographic opportunities from all positions on the boat.

OUT OF THE BLUE

Introducing the location: Cardigan Bay is the UK's first *Marine Heritage Coast* and is a magical place of towering cliffs and rolling sand dunes. Your home for this holiday is the charming harbour town of New Quay, overlooking the bay. The second destination is Pembrokeshire, staying in Britain's smallest city, St Davids, situated within the Pembrokeshire Coast National Park.

Species: In Cardigan Bay, you will see Common Bottlenose Dolphins, Risso's Dolphins and Harbour Porpoises as well as a variety of seabird populations. Pembrokeshire is frequented by schools of Short-beaked Common Dolphins, often in their hundreds, sometimes in their thousands. Other possibilities include Northern Minke Whale, Common Bottlenose Dolphin and, for the very lucky, Killer Whale.

Trip details: The Cardigan Bay trip includes coastal walks, shore-based dolphin watching and relaxing afternoon boat trips. The Pembrokeshire trip involves several boat trips on a comfortable boat and a day trip to Skomer Island for close up encounters with Puffins and other seabirds.

Operating season: May - August.

Price: Cardigan Bay (4 days): adults £399, children (under 14 years) £325. Pembrokeshire (6 days): adults £649.

Departure time and duration: Vessels are chartered for the holidays. They leave during the day, with most excursions lasting between two and six hours.

Departure location and how to get there: *Out of the Blue* travellers are given dossiers detailing meeting and departure times for all boat trips.

Naturalist guides: Tours are accompanied by a *Whale and Dolphin Conservation Society* representative, along with a local guide with in-depth knowledge of the area.

Vessel details: Cardigan Bay excursions take place onboard the *Sulaire*, a modern boat with an excellent viewing platform.
   Pembrokeshire expeditions are onboard the *Ocean Ranger*, a powerful twin engine vessel ideal for watching wildlife.

Photographic opportunities: Weather permitting, both trips offer fantastic photographic opportunities from both the land and the sea.

Conservation / Research: *Out of the Blue* donates a percentage of profit to *WDCS* which goes directly to funding its vital conservation work.

Location: Pembrokeshire / New Quay

Name of operator: Out of the Blue

Website: www. wdcs.org/outoftheblue

Telephone: 01249 449533 / 547

Fax: 01249 449501

E-mail: outoftheblue@ wdcs.org

Address: Brookfield House, 38 St Pauls Street, Chippenham, Wiltshire, SN15 1LJ

Photography: © Rob Lott

Boat-based Listing

SEALIFE ADVENTURES

Introducing the location: Cruise through the infamous Corryvreckan Whirlpool and enjoy the stunning panorama of islands such as Mull, Iona, Jura and Islay whilst searching for whales, dolphins, porpoises and other wildlife.

Species: This area is a hot spot for Harbour Porpoise, Northern Minke Whale, dolphins and Basking Sharks, as well as Otters, seals, deer and many birds.

Trip details: The two hour cruise is a fun-packed sprint to the Corryvreckan whirlpool. The three hour cruise also features the Corryvreckan whirlpool but covers a larger area, with more time spent with the wildlife. To the west of the Corryvreckan the route follows the 'Great Race'- an offshore tidal stream in which sightings of Northern Minke Whales are frequent. The four hour landing trip stops at the southernmost island of the Garvellachs chain to explore the fascinating ruins that were built by the early Scots almost 1500 years ago. The five hour cruise is a dedicated whale watching trip, heading out through the Corryvreckan to the open seas in search of Northern Minke Whales. Expect to see all the variety of wildlife this *Special Area of Conservation* has to offer, including dolphins, Harbour Porpoises and many seabirds.

Operating season: All year.

Price: Two hour trips: adult £28.50, child (under 16) £19.75. Three hour trips: adult £39.00, child £29.00. Four hour trips: adult £49.50, child £39.50. Five hour offshore whale watching: adult £55.00, child £45.00. See website for details of family and group discounts.

Departure time and duration: Please see the 'trip calendar' on the website for details.

Departure location and how to get there: Approximately eight miles south of Oban on the A816, turn on to the B844 signposted for Isle of Seil and the 'Atlantic Bridge'. Follow the B844 on to and along Seil Island. Turn left immediately after the golf course at the junction, following the road through Balvicar village and on to Balvicar pier. In 2008 departure point may change to a mile closer to Oban.

Naturalist guides: Ruth, the wildlife guide, has a degree in biology. She will also serve tea, chocolate, coffee and biscuits.

Vessel details: The purpose-built *Porpoise II* - with nearly 900 horse power it is Britain's most powerful wildlife charter boat, offering unparalleled stability, safety and comfort.

Photographic opportunities: Excellent. The skipper, David, is a keen photographer and videographer, and has provided footage for a number of television productions.

Conservation / Research: Sightings are submitted to the *Hebridean Whale and Dolphin Trust*. David also serves on the *Firth of Lorn Special Area of Conservation Management Committee.*

Location:
Dunaverty, Argyll

Name of operator:
Sealife-adventures

Website: www.
sealife-adventures
.com

Telephone:
01631 571010
(office hours),
01852 300203
(evenings and
weekends)

Fax:
01852 300203

E-mail:
info@sealife-
adventures.com

Address:
Dunaverty, Easdale,
By Oban, Argyll,
PA34 4RF

Boat-based Listing

SEA.FARI ADVENTURES

Introducing the location: Cross the infamous Bridge over the Atlantic to the Isle of Seil and the conservation village of Easdale, 16 miles south of Oban. Easdale was once the centre of the Scottish slate industry and is now a conservation area.

Species: Harbour Porpoise, Common Bottlenose Dolphin, Northern Minke Whale, Basking Shark, Ocean Sunfish, Otter, seals and much more. Land-based wildlife includes Red Deer and Golden Eagle.

Trip details: A range of tours including numerous encounters with cetaceans and a host of wildlife in natural surroundings within the European *Special Area of Conservation,* Firth of Lorne. Visit the Gulf of Corryvreckan, home to the world's third largest whirlpool. Harbour Porpoise and Common Bottlenose Dolphin sightings throughout the year. Northern Minke Whale from late April / early May to mid October. *Sea.fari Adventures (Oban)* operates three boats from Easdale. The crew are aware of cetacean movements in the area, ensuring the best viewing opportunities for customers. Tours are designed to be interactive, with private charters for the dedicated wildlife enthusiast, including landing trips with guided tours to points of interest.

Operating season: Daily from Easter to November. Also limited winter sailings.

Price: depends on tour, family, and group discounts. See website or phone for details.

Departure time and duration: Departure times vary according to season and tides; please phone for details. Duration from one hour to full day excursions.

Departure location and how to get there: From Oban take the A816 south and turn right on to the B844 signposted Easdale. Follow the brown Sea.fari tourist signs from the A816.

Naturalist guides: All Skippers are *WiSe (Wildlife Safe operator accredited)* with many years' experience. Crew are generally post-graduates with related degree, some with many years' professional guiding experience.

Vessel details: 3 x 10m rigid-hulled inflatable boats with twin 250hp engines. Full safety certificates. Boats designed and built in the company's own workshops specifically for wildlife watching. All vessels operate with skipper and dedicated crew. Individual passenger seats including parent / child seats. Maximum of 12 passengers per boat.

Photographic opportunities: Excellent. Cameras and binoculars carried at own risk.

Conservation / Research: All cetacean sightings are recorded and made available to responsible bodies.

Location:
Easdale, Argyll

Name of operator:
Sea.fari Adventures
(Oban)

Website:
www.seafari.co.uk

Telephone:
01852 300003

Fax:
01852 300341

E-mail:
oban@seafari.co.uk

Address:
Sea.fari Adventures,
Easdale, Oban,
Argyll. Scotland,
PA34 4RF

Boat-based Listing

SEA LIFE SURVEYS

Introducing the location: For the past 15 years *Sea Life Surveys* have been successfully operating specialist wildlife trips in the fascinating and exciting waters around Mull, Coll, Muck, Eigg, Rum and the Treshnish Isles. The rugged isles and clean seas provide the perfect environment for the wildlife to flourish and the sea area supports a huge abundance of breeding birds, seals, otters, whales, dolphins and Harbour Porpoises to name a few.

Species: Minke Whale, Harbour Porpoise, and several species of dolphin, Basking Shark, and a large variety of seabirds.

Trip details: Three boats offering a great variety of wildlife cruises to suit all ages and levels of experience.

Operating season: All year.

Price: ranging from £6 to £70 per person.

Departure time and duration: ranging from a 30 minute cruise to eight hour cruises.

Departure location and how to get there: All cruises depart from Tobermory. There are regular ferry sailings from Oban on the mainland (40 minutes) run by Caledonian Macbrayne - Tel: 01631 566688. Web: www.calmac.co.uk.

Naturalist guides: All cruises have experienced wildlife guides on board.

Vessel details: *Sula Bheag* – 15m purpose-built passenger vessel – up to 40 people. *Sula Mhor* – 16m passenger vessel – up to 40 people.

Photographic opportunities: The Inner Hebrides is just one large photographic opportunity. Large range of wildlife, magical scenery, ever-changing colours of the Atlantic seascape and, of course, the wildlife.

Conservation / Research: Every passenger on every cruise contributes directly in assisting with marine research that was established 20 years ago.

Location:
Isle of Mull, Argyll

Name of operator:
Sea Life Surveys

Website: www.sealifesurveys.com

Telephone:
01688 302916 / 302038

E-mail: info@sealifesurveys.com

Address:
Ledaig, Tobermory, Isle of Mull, PA75 6NR

Boat-based Listing

ARDNAMURCHAN POINT

Introduction: Ardnamurchan Point forms the most westerly promontory in mainland Britain. It affords spectacular views across the Hebrides to the Isle of Mull, the Small Isles of Eigg, Muck and Rhum, the Isle of Skye and the islands of Canna, Coll and Tiree. On clear days the Outer Hebrides are also visible.

Species and season: Northern Minke Whales are regularly seen between April and September. Harbour Porpoise, Common Bottlenose Dolphin, Short-beaked Common Dolphin and Risso's Dolphin are also sighted with some regularity, with the very occasional

group of Killer Whales passing by. Other regular visitors include Basking Shark, Otter and both Common and Atlantic Grey Seals.

How to get there: Ardnamurchan Point is at the western tip of the Ardnamurchan peninsula. From Fort William, take the A830 west to Lochailort. From here, take the A861 south to Salen, then follow the B8007 west across Ardnamurchan to the lighthouse.

Facilities: There is a lighthouse, visitor centre, coffee shop, gift shop, and toilets.

Location:
Ardnamurchan
Point, Argyll

Contact:
The
Ardnamurchan
Lighthouse Trust,
Ardnamurchan
Point, Kilchoan,
Acharacle, Argyll,
Scotland,
PH36 4LN

Telepone:
01972 510210

Fax:
01972 510396

E-mail: davie@
ardnamurchan.u-
net.com.

Website: www.
ardnamurchan.u-
net.com.

Photography:
© John Young

Land-based Listing

HEBRIDEAN WHALE CRUISES

Introducing the location: The waters around Gairloch are well recognised for their cetacean sightings. Gairloch is a picturesque fishing village surrounded by the Torridon mountain ranges.

Species: Northern Minke Whale, Harbour Porpoise, Short-beaked Common Dolphin, and Risso's Dolphin frequently sighted. Occasional visitors include Common Bottlenose, White-beaked and Atlantic White-sided Dolphin, Humpback, Fin, Sei, Sperm, Long-finned Pilot, Killer, and Northern Bottlenose Whale.

Trip details: One to three hour cruises, including Shiant Island cruises and offshore whale and pelagic bird spotting.

Operating season: All year.

Price: From £12 to £47.50 depending on the vessel and duration.

Departure time and duration: Dependent upon demand and forecasted weather.

Departure location and how to get there: Gairloch is on the A837 coast road between Ullapool and Kyle of Lochalsh. Trips depart from Gairloch Pier.

Naturalist guides: The guide is a marine zoologist.

Vessel details: Two vessels. *Mitchell,* a 31ft wide-beamed Sea Angler with full weatherproof sheltered deck, and an 11m offshore rigid-hulled inflatable boat. Flotation suits provided.

Photographic opportunities: Wildlife and scenery, including the Shiant Islands.

Conservation and Research: Hebridean Whale Cruises have developed a photographic catalogue for individuals of Northern Minke Whale, Common Bottlenose Dolphin, and Killer Whale, along with the only Risso's Dolphin database in Great Britain.

Location: Gairloch

Name of operator: Hebridean Whale Cruises

Website: www.hebridean-whale-cruises.com

Telephone: 01445 712458

Fax: 01445 712458

E-mail: nick999davies@ hotmail.com

Address: Gairloch Chandlery and Wildlife Centre, Pier Road. Gairloch, Wester Ross, IV21 2BP

Boat-based Listing

RUA REIDH LIGHTHOUSE

Introduction: Rua Reidh Lighthouse is situated in the heart of Scotland's wild west coast. The approach road and headland offer superb views westwards across the Minch. It is also possible to stay at the lighthouse, which has been converted into a bed and breakfast hostel.

Species and season: Summer and autumn are the best months to visit as calmer weather conditions prevail. Harbour Porpoises and Basking Sharks are common, whilst Northern Minke Whales and Short-beaked Common Dolphins are seen regularly. The lucky observer may even encounter a White-beaked Dolphin or Killer Whale. The coastline here is also good for Otters and White-tailed Sea Eagles.

How to get there: After reaching Gairloch, continue through the village for a mile before turning left by the Police Station on to a road signposted to Melvaig. Continue along this road for 13 miles to Rua Reidh. The last three miles are very slow as the road is narrow and winding.

Facilities: None (unless you are staying at the lighthouse).

Location:
Rua Reidh
Lighthouse,
Ross-shire

Contact:
Rua Reidh
Lighthouse,
Melvaig, Gairloch,
Ross-shire,
IV21 2EA.

Telephone:
01445 771263

E-mail: ruareidh@
tiscali.co.uk

Photography:
Northern Minke
Whale
© Alex Carlisle

WiSe whale and dolphin wildlife watching

Nothing can beat the experience of seeing some of our most wonderful marine life at close quarters – whales and dolphins. And, naturally, it is of the greatest importance that these animals we care so much about are not disturbed by our presence – that's where the skill and concern of your boat crew are of the greatest importance.

What is WiSe?

WiSe is a Training and Accreditation programme for Commercial boat skippers and their crews, in which techniques are presented for safe and sustainable viewing of marine wildlife (whales and dolphins, basking sharks, seals and seabirds). Each individual attends a one-day course, presented by instructors with many years of experience in both marine ecotourism and research. Accreditation of the individual lasts for three years, and can be renewed by attending an update course, to ensure that all operators are kept informed of the latest changes in the Law relating to wildlife, and new discoveries about behaviour, for example, from scientific studies around the world.

How do I find a WiSe Accredited operator?

The *WiSe* website (www.wisescheme.org) lists all of the Companies who have had staff Accredited. Over the last three years courses have been run in southwest England, Wales, the Isle of Man, Northern Ireland and Scotland, with nearly five hundred individuals attending. Most of them will be found on the website. Contact details for Companies, details of where and when they operate from, what you might see and, in most cases links to their website are all features of the *WiSe* website.

WiSe up!

The individuals who have attended the WiSe courses spend considerable amounts of time around our precious marine life, and know how important it is to employ sustainable techniques to ensure the long-term well-being of these creatures. This is why they have chosen to attend a *WiSe* course, to learn and exchange views on sustainable wildlife watching. So if you are planning to visit our coast, then a good place to start your journey is via our website, and to find out what is on offer at your destination. The waters around Britain offer huge rewards in terms of sensational wildlife sights – help to ensure that will always be the case by choosing to see them first hand with a *WiSe* trained and Accredited Operator.

Room 14
Falmouth Marine School
Killigrew Street
Falmouth TR11 3QS
Tel: 01326 313886
E-Mail
info@wisescheme.org
Website
www.wisescheme.org

TIUMPAN HEAD

Introduction: Situated on the Eye Peninsula north east of Stornoway, Tiumpan Head forms the most easterly point of the Isle of Lewis, facing eastwards over the waters of the Minch. Watch from the car park at the lighthouse, which is also an excellent picnic location. There is also an excellent viewpoint at the top of the hill, which is accessible by a good path.

Species and season: Water depths in excess of 100m occur in a natural trench close inshore here, providing suitable habitat for a diversity of cetaceans. Tiumpan's speciality species is the Risso's Dolphin, which is present year-round in the area. During the summer months when calmer weather makes watching easier, White-beaked Dolphins, Harbour Porpoises and Northern Minke Whales are also regularly seen. Occasional species include Atlantic White-sided Dolphin, Long-finned Pilot Whale and Killer Whale, whilst Fin, Sei, Humpback and Sperm Whales pass by on rare occasions.

How to get there: Tiumpan Head is around 12 miles from Stornoway. Follow the A866 Stornoway to Broker road past the airport and into Point district. Once in Broker, the top of the lighthouse can be seen straight ahead.

Facilities: There are no facilities, apart from the picnic area. The nearest public toilets are at Bayble beach, about half way between Stornoway and Broker.

Contact:
Stornoway Tourist Information Centre, 26 Cromwell Street, Stornoway, Isle of Lewis, HS1 2DD

Telephone:
01851 703088

Fax:
01851 705244

Photography:
Risso's Dolphin
© Alex Carlisle

Land-based Listing

SUMBURGH HEAD

Introduction: Sumburgh Head is a towering outcrop of rock rising magnificently at the southern tip of Mainland Shetland. The beautiful lighthouse at its summit was designed by Robert Stevenson and dates back to 1821. Today, Sumburgh Head is managed by the Royal Society for the Protection of Birds because it hosts thousands of breeding Puffins, Guillemots, Shags and Fulmars. Sumburgh Head is positioned at the meeting point of the North Sea and the Atlantic Ocean, and the resulting mixing of the waters produces a nutrient rich soup resulting in a proliferation of marine creatures that are preyed upon by seabirds and cetaceans.

Species and season: Between May and mid August Sumburgh Head is at its vibrant best, with spectacular seabird colonies and a good chance of cetaceans on calmer days. Binoculars and a telescope are useful allies when watching from these 100m high cliffs, but the rewards can be outstanding. Harbour Porpoises, White-beaked Dolphins and Northern Minke Whales are regularly sighted, and rarities have included Humpback Whales and large pods of Atlantic White-sided Dolphins. Somewhat easier to see are the Atlantic Grey Seals that haul out daily at the base of the cliffs.

Sumburgh Head also has the enviable reputation as the best place in Britain to look for Killer Whales from land. Whilst they are always unpredictable, several groups circle the islands each summer to hunt the Common and Atlantic Grey Seals that breed throughout the region. Sightings of Killer Whales vary from year to year, but occur year-round, peaking in June. Views can be outstanding as the animals often occur within a few metres of shore as they seek out their prey.

How to get there: Take the A970 from Lerwick heading south. Pass the airport on your left and continue past Grutness for just over a mile until you reach the Sumburgh Head car park. There is excellent viewing eastwards from the car park, but it is also worth taking the steep path to the lighthouse to view cliff nesting birds and the sea south west towards Fair Isle. For less mobile visitors there is a small disabled car park near the lighthouse.

For recent sightings news or to report your own sightings in the Shetland Islands, contact Hugh Harrop, Cetacean Recorder, Shetland Sea Mammal Group, c/o Shetland Wildlife, Longhill, Maywick, Shetland, ZE2 9JF. Tel: 01950 422483. Email: info@shetlandwildlife.co.uk

Location:
Sumburgh Head,
Shetland

Contact:
RSPB Sumburgh
Head Nature
Reserve, East
House, Sumburgh
Head Lighthouse,
Virkie, Shetland,
ZE3 9JN

Telephone:
01950 460800

Photography:
© Ian Broadbent

Land-based Listing

OUT OF THE BLUE

Introducing the location: The Moray Firth is a beautiful and unspoilt region in the north of Scotland. This trip is based in the town of Cromarty, one of the most stunning towns in the Highlands. A short distance from Cromarty is Chanonry Point where, if conditions are right, you should be able to see dolphins just metres from the shore. On the west coast the tour heads to Gairloch to take in the rugged land and seascapes of Loch Ewe and the Shiant Islands.

Species: Common Bottlenose Dolphin and Harbour Porpoise in the Moray Firth. In Gairloch, regular visitors to the area include Northern Minke Whale, Short-beaked Common, Common Bottlenose and Risso's Dolphins, Killer Whale, Basking Shark and both Common and Atlantic Grey Seals.

Location:
The Moray Firth /
Gairloch

Name of operator:
Out of the Blue

Website: www.
wdcs.org/outoftheblue

Telephone:
01249 449533 /
449547

Fax:
01249 449501

E-mail:
outoftheblue@
wdcs.org

Address:
Brookfield House,
38 St Pauls Street,
Chippenham,
Wiltshire, SN15 1LJ

Photography:
© Charlie Phillips

Trip details: The Moray Firth holiday includes a day trip to the *Whale and Dolphin Conservation Society*'s (*WDCS*) Wildlife Centre, leisurely boat cruises and a picturesque coastal walk. The Gairloch holiday is a wildlife photographer's dream. Charlie Phillips, *WDCS* field officer and professional photographer, will be on hand to show you how to make the most of the fantastic array of wildlife and scenery on offer.

Operating season:
May - September.

Price: Short break (4 days): adults £399, children (under 14 years) £325. Gairloch (6 days): adults £699, children (under 12 years) £550.

Departure time and duration: Vessels are chartered for the holidays. Most boat trips last between two and four hours, although some are full day excursions.

Departure location and how to get there: *Out of the Blue* travellers are given dossiers detailing meeting and departure times for all boat trips.

Naturalist guides: A *WDCS* representative along with a local guide with in-depth knowledge of the area.

Vessel details: *The Starquest, Saorsa* and the *Gemini Explorer* are all vessels with an experienced and responsible crew.

Photographic opportunities: All trips offer fantastic photographic opportunities from both the land and the sea.

Conservation / Research: *Out of the Blue* donates a percentage of profit to *WDCS* which goes directly to funding its vital conservation work.

MORAY FIRTH

Location: Moray Firth, North East Scotland

Introduction: Not only is the Moray Firth one of the best locations to watch Common Bottlenose Dolphins from commercial tour boats, there are also some outstanding dolphin watching locations along the shore, with dolphins regularly occurring within a few metres of the beach in some places.

First prize here must go to Chanonry Point - an idyllic spot situated where the Firth narrows dramatically. Two hours before high tide, rapid currents push through this 'bottleneck', concentrating prey close to shore. The dolphins are seen daily here, often performing acrobatics to the delight of onlooking crowds. On the opposite side of the Firth here is Fort George, which is also excellent for close views. Several of the other best places to watch also involve narrow channels of water where rapid tidal currents create optimum feeding conditions. They include the North and South Sutors, which guard the entrance to the Cromarty Firth, and North and South Kessock, which overlook the entrance to the Beauly Firth at Inverness. Dolphins are also regularly sighted from headlands and bays along the south coast of the Firth, including Findhorn, Burghead, Lossiemouth, Spey Bay and Portknockie.

Species and season: Common Bottlenose Dolphins are the main attraction in the Moray Firth. Sightings of these dolphins in the Inner Moray Firth are strongly influenced by the tide. Try to refer to a tide table before planning your

Location:
Moray Firth, North
East Scotland

Photography:
Dolphins breaching
at Chanonary Point
© Charlie Phillips

Land-based Listing

watching, as animals are much more likely to be present during the three hours either side of high tide.

Harbour Porpoises and Northern Minke Whales are also regularly seen, particularly in the Outer Firth to the east. Rarities have included Killer Whale, Humpback Whale and Northern Bottlenose Whale, and White-beaked Dolphins are probably more common offshore than sightings suggest. The Moray Firth is also famous amongst cetacean scholars as the location where Sowerby's Beaked Whale became known to science. A specimen was discovered stranded in 1800 and described four years later by water-colour artist James Sowerby.

How to get there: Inverness is the obvious starting point for a day's dolphin watching in the Moray Firth. Why not start at the edge of town at South Kessock, or cross the Kessock Bridge and watch from the other side? Heading north on the A9, take the

A832 east onto the Black Isle. Turn right at Rosemarkie for Chanonry Point, passing a golf course and arriving at a car park by the quaint lighthouse. Continuing northwards on the A832 leads to Cromarty and the Sutors – another hotspot. Alternatively, skirt the southern side of the Firth by taking the A96 road to the east of Inverness and stopping off at Findhorn, Burghead, Lossiemouth, Spey Bay and Portknockie. The dolphins tend to be more distant from along this stretch of coast, although some elevated viewpoints at Burghead and Lossiemouth make it easier to view larger areas of sea or spot fins between the waves.

Photographic opportunities: Excellent opportunities for using cameras with long lenses and mounted on tripods, particularly at North Kessock and Chanonry Point, where dolphins are frequently demonstrative and spend time close to shore.

Photography:
© Charlie Phillips

Land-based Listing

GIRDLENESS

Introduction: Girdleness is situated in the heart of the city of Aberdeen where the River Dee reaches the sea at the city's docks. It's a surprisingly peaceful place, with lots of green space for a pleasant walk. Alternatively, find a good view of the harbour mouth and, with patience, you could be watching dolphins.

Species and season: Bottlenose Dolphins are sighted regularly throughout the year both inside and outside the harbour mouth, often performing acrobatic leaps. In the bay, Harbour Porpoises are also present year-round, whilst Northern Minke Whales and White-beaked Dolphins are seen irregularly during the summer and autumn. Rarities have included Short-beaked Common Dolphin, Atlantic White-sided Dolphin, Killer Whale, Humpback Whale and Fin Whale.

How to get there: Turn off the A956 towards Torry and follow Greyhope Road along the south side of the river towards the harbour mouth and around Nigg Bay Golf Club (Balnagask Golf Course). Park at the large unsurfaced car park on a rise to the right of the road, at the remains of Torry Battery, to look over the harbour mouth. Continuing along Greyhope Road, a good panorama (and shelter from the wind) can be found at the foghorn below Girdleness Lighthouse.

Location:
Girdleness,
Aberdeen

Photography:
© Alex Wilson /
WildPics.org

Land-based Listing

Dolphin Space Programme

The Moray Firth in north east Scotland supports the only bottlenose dolphin population in the North Sea. It is one of the best places in UK waters for watching dolphins, whales, porpoises, seals and seabirds, from land or sea.

The **Dolphin Space Programme** (DSP) is a training and accreditation scheme for wildlife tour boats in the Moray Firth which promotes and supports responsible, sustainable marine wildlife tourism.

DSP accredited tour boats follow a code of conduct to avoid causing disturbance to dolphins and other marine wildlife.

DSP accredited boats act responsibly around cetaceans and allow the animals to choose how they want to interact with the boat. DSP operators offer a high quality, enjoyable wildlife experience taking in the natural beauty of the Moray Firth.

The DSP is funded by Scottish Natural Heritage (SNH), the Whale and Dolphin Conservation Society (WDCS) and the Moray Firth Partnership and is overseen by a steering group comprising VisitScotland, the Wildlife Tour Boat Operators' Society, WDCS, the Northern Constabulary, Grampian Police, The Highland Council, Inverness Harbour Trust, the Maritime Coastguard Agency and SNH.

SCOTTISH
NATURAL
HERITAGE
DUALCHAS
NADAIR
na h-ALBA

WDCS
Whale and Dolphin Conservation Society

MORAY FIRTH PARTNERSHIP

For more information, operator contact details or help with booking your trip please visit our website at **www.dolphinspace.org** or contact the Project Officer on email: **projectofficer@dolphinspace.org** or by post: **DSP, P.O. Box 5890, Forres, Moray,**

OTHER BOAT OPERATORS

North East England

DFDS Seaways
(Newcastle – Stavanger /
Haugesund / Bergen route)
International Ferry Terminal
Royal Quays
North Shields
Tyne and Wear, NE29 6EE
Telephone: 0871 5229955
Website:
www.dfds.co.uk/dsw/en

South East England and the Channel Islands

P&O Ferries
(Portsmouth – Bilbao route)
Channel House
Channel View Road
Dover
CT17 9TJ
Telephone: 08705 980333
Email:
customer.services@poferries.com
Website:
www.poferries.com/tourist/

South West England

Brittany Ferries
(Plymouth – Santander route)
Millbay
Plymouth
Devon
England
PL1 3EW
Telephone: 0870 9076103
Website:
www.brittany-ferries.co.uk

Scillonian III Ferry
(Penzance – Isles of Scilly)
Isles of Scilly Steamship

Group
Steamship House
Quay Street
Penzance
Cornwall
TR18 4BD
Telephone:
01736 362009 / 362124
Website:
www.chycor.co.uk/tourism/issc
/steamship.htm

Wales

Irish Ferries
(Holyhead – Dublin route,
Pembroke – Rosslare route)
Holyhead Port
Salt Island
Holyhead
Gwynedd
LL65 1DR
Pembroke Port
Pembroke Dock
Pembrokeshire
SA72 6TW
Telephone: 08705 171717
Website:
www.irishferries.com/

Thousand Islands Expeditions
Cross Square
St Davids
SA62 6SL.
Telephone: 01437 721721 /
721686
Website:
www.thousandislands.co.uk

Venture Jet Limited
Llanon
Trefin
Haverfordwest
Pembrokeshire

SA62 5AE
Telephone: 01348 837764
Freephone: 08000 854786
Website:
www.venturejet.co.uk

Scotland

Caledonian MacBrayne Ferries
(Western Scotland to the
Western Isles)
Ferry Terminal
Gourock
PA19 1QP
Telephone: 01475 650100
Website:
www.calmac.co.uk/

Dolphin Trips Avoch
Harbour Office
Pierhead
Avoch
Ross-Shire
IV9 8PT
Telephone: 01381 622383
Website:
www.dolphintripsavoch.co.uk

Arisaig Marine Ltd
The Harbour
Arisaig
Inverness-shire
PH39 4NH
Telephone: 01687 450224
Website: www.arisaig.co.uk

EcoVentures
Harbour Place
Cromarty
IV11 8YE
Tel: 01381 600323
Website: www.ecoventures.co.uk

Gairloch Marine Life Centre and Cruises
Charleston Harbour
Pier Road
Gairloch
Ross-shire
IV21 2BQ
Telephone: 01445 712636
Website: www.porpoise-gairloch.co.uk

Inter Island Ferry Service
(Shetland Mainland –
Fair Isle)
Shetland Island Council
Town hall
UpperHillhead
Lenwick
Shetland
ZE1 0HB
Tel: 01595 760222
Website: www.shetland.gov.uk/ferries

Guideliner Hebridean Wildlife Cruises
Erne Lodge
Kingsborough
Snizort
Isle of Skye
IV51 9UT
Telphone: 01470 532393
Website: www.guideliner.co.uk

Look out for upcoming whale and dolphin
guides from CETACEA Publishing.
Full details will be posted on our website
www.cetaceapublishing.com

M.V. Volante
Thistledo
Iona
Argyll
PA76 6SP
Telephone: 01681 700 362
Website: www.volanteiona.com

North 58 Sea Adventures
8 Quayside
Banff
Aberdeenshire
AB45 1HQ
Telephone: 01261 819900
Mobile: 07854 447720
Website: www.north58.co.uk

Northcoast Marine Adventures
Longfield
Dunnet
By Thurso
KW14 8YD
Telephone: 01955 611797
Website: www.northcoast.fsnet.co.uk

Puffin Cruises
Macduff
Scotland
Telephone: 01542 832560
Mobile: 07900 920445
Website: www.puffincruises.co.uk

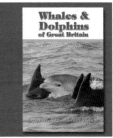
Boat-based Listings

TIPS AND TRICKS FOR PHOTOGRAPHERS

Photographing any wild animals can be extremely difficult as, unlike photographing a pet, you cannot ask it to "stay", "sit" or "wait"! Consequently it is necessary to try and follow a few basic rules to help you get the best from your photography.

Getting out on the water to meet dolphins or even whales in the wild can be a life changing experience. Even for experienced whale watchers and researchers, seeing a new species or having an encounter with an animal that they recognise can be an incredible thrill. The authors of this book have taken several thousand photographs of cetaceans, both for recreational and research purposes. Whilst we certainly don't claim to have all the answers to taking pictures in a difficult environment, we would like to offer you our top 10 tips to taking good photographs of cetaceans.

1. The first decision to make with any photography is what equipment to buy? We recommend a digital Single Lens Reflex (SLR) camera with an image stabilising lens. We generally favour a 70-300mm lens, which is very good as it is not too cumbersome to use on a boat but also gives you the opportunity of getting good images of cetaceans at a range of distances. Remember that such cameras are heavy and you may have them around your neck for a number of hours, so make sure your equipment is comfortable to wear.

2. Remain patient. It can be very exciting when dolphins or whales are around, but don't be too quick to fire off shots as soon as animals are spotted. They may be several hundred metres away and, whilst they may look big through your binoculars, when you later view pictures taken at this distance you could be disappointed to find a selection of seascapes and dots! As a general rule, try and wait until your target is within 100m of the boat. This is not to say that more distant sightings are of no value to the photographer (see tip 3).

3. Put down your camera at some point during the encounter (particularly when the animals are distant) and take time to study them and understand their movements and behaviour. This will improve your chances of taking good photographs should they approach closely.

4. The big challenge for any cetacean photographer is to try to work out where the animals will surface next and attempt to line the camera up on that spot. Positioning yourself high up on the vessel will make it easier for you to spot animals under the water just before they surface.

5. If your camera has a sports setting or the option of a fast shutter speed, use it. By using shutter speeds in excess of 1000th of a second, you are more likely to obtain images with your target in focus.

6. If the cetaceans are moving rapidly, try pre-focusing on the sea surface where you expect your animal to rise. This way, if the cetacean is on the surface for a short time, you don't miss the opportunity due to the time it takes for your camera to focus (note that, in certain conditions, your camera may struggle to focus

Fin Whale © hughharrop.com

on the water due to its reflective quality).

7. On a clear day, remember to position yourself in relation to the sun. Shooting into the sun can create some very artistic effects but your subject is likely to be silhouetted. For detailed cetacean pictures, shoot with the sun behind you. Early morning and evening are generally the best times for such photography. Cloudy days can also produce surprisingly good photographic results, as there is no glare from the sun. Photographing pale species, such as Risso's Dolphin, on dull days also reduces the risk of over-exposing the image.

8. Although digital cameras are very good for a number of different applications, they can be frustratingly slow at taking pictures in some situations. Taking images at a smaller file size will enable you to take more images at once (on motor drive), but will also compromise the quality of that 'once-in-a-lifetime' photograph. Changing the camera setting to video is an alternative option if you have an instant camera, as you can still grab a still image from the video footage when you get home.

9. Make sure you have more than enough film or memory cards and always allow for the unexpected. There is nothing worse than the realisation that you have run out of options just as a whale starts to breach. We recommend 512mb or 1gb memory cards for digital cameras.

10. Be indulgent. To get good whale images you need to shoot a lot of frames. Remember, it is normal to take a lot of pictures of waves and splashes before you get your first outstanding whale or dolphin image!

All photography with copyright
breathtakingwhales.com **or** *WildPics.org*
can be purchased from the publishers.
Tel: 0845 388 3053. Pictures can be
supplied for personal useage or
commercial use.

Cameras ready, whales surfacing © Alex Wilson / WildPics.org with a boat. Wild cetaceans are often interested in socialising with vessels, but they also need time to themselves. This is very evident when they are feeding, nurturing young or even travelling. It is essential to try and understand dolphins and whales when approaching them; something that comes with experience.

"Many people are amazed to learn about the diversity of cetacean species in the waters around Britain and Ireland," says Vanessa Williams-Grey, from the *Whale and Dolphin Conservation Society.*

"You really can't beat our waters when it comes to diversity and opportunities for viewing from land as well as from the sea! Common Bottlenose Dolphins are resident off west Wales and north-east Scotland, whilst Harbour Porpoises, Short-beaked Common, White-beaked and Risso's Dolphins, and even larger species including Northern Minke, Long-finned Pilot, Humpback and Fin, and Killer Whales, may also be found. If you take a boat trip, do a bit of research first and select a trip which

abides by relevant regulations and codes of conduct (in the Moray Firth, look out for operators accredited by the *Dolphin Space Programme (DSP)*, and operators trained and accredited under the *Wildlife Safe (WiSe)* scheme." Cetaceans can be easily disturbed – even harmed – by a vessel which is handled without proper care, so it is vital to make sure that all vessels engaged in viewing marine wildlife do so in a manner that is thoughtful and responsible."

Commercial whale and dolphin watching is a multi-billion dollar industry worldwide. This has led to a number of countries and areas adopting proper regulations to help both the commercial fleets and private boat owners alike. One man who has spent years developing regulations and codes of conduct for whale watching boats in his home waters as well as in other countries is Greg Kauffman, the president and founder of the *Pacific Whale Foundation* in Hawaii. This organisation carries out whale and dolphin research in a number of countries

Bending the rules - a young Humpback Whale approaches a whale watching boat in Queensland, Australia © Alex Wilson / WildPics.org

Responsible Whale Watching

around the world, including Hawaii and Australia.

Kauffman recalls that, "back in the 1980s, Hawaii residents and the *Pacific Whale Foundation* petitioned the government to regulate approaches to whales. Our island boaters were right there with us, pushing for these limits. Resulting Federal and State regulations made it illegal to approach whales, by any means, within 100 yards in Hawaii's waters. Aircraft also had to comply, by maintaining a 1,000 foot flight bubble around whales.

"Today, there is a high rate of compliance with boaters; and indeed many boaters are looking at additional ways they can help protect the whales. In recent years, the *Pacific Whale Foundation* has conducted a series of workshops for boat operators to develop additional voluntary guidelines for handling vessels around whales."

Here in the UK the *WiSe* scheme operates courses for skippers of whale watching vessels to get a fuller understanding of the correct way to whale and dolphin watch. These courses are run at various places and once completed, the skipper is able to say that they are *WiSe* accredited, and the company is able to display the *WiSe* logo on their literature and vessels. Recreational boat owners and skippers have also attended some of these courses and we heard from Colin Speedie, the director of the scheme, that they have also produced a DVD in conjunction with the *Royal Yachting Association*

as a further way of distributing these guidelines.

"All of us love to see whales and dolphins in the wild," explains Speedie, "but, if we are not careful when viewing them we may cause them harm. Careful boat handling and an awareness that the sea is their world, not ours, can help to minimise that risk, and safeguard them for future generations to enjoy."

Cardigan Bay Marine Wildlife Centre works alongside a local charter vessel, taking customers to see the dolphins whilst collecting data for the centre. We spoke to the Centre manager and experienced whale watch skipper, Steve Hartley;

"My feelings about boat owners where cetacean watching is concerned is that, as our local commercial code of conduct states, the public should not approach the animals but stop, watch the animals at a safe distance, and then carry on their way, allowing the dolphins to approach the boats if they wish. This leaves the choice to the animals, letting them initiate the encounter. I would be concerned if the general public were to be encouraged to approach groups of cetaceans even at appropriate angles etc., as I am sure this would lead to unwitting harassment and disturbance. For example, often dolphin behaviour can be misinterpreted. People can be heard to say how the dolphins love to bow-ride. When harassed and disturbed they might briefly do this but often as a reaction to being disturbed from social, feeding and other behaviours to which they would have been much better off being left alone".

© Charlie Phillips

Responsible Whale Watching

Whale and dolphin watching on land, on a ferry, on a specialist trip, or on your own boat is incredibly rewarding, but it must be carried out responsibly. The information or photographs you take may well be helpful to researchers to further their understanding of cetaceans in our waters; so find out locally who can benefit from your data and pictures.

Margaux Dodds, director and co-founder of the *Marine Connection* explains,

"Seeing dolphins or whales in their natural environment gives the ideal opportunity to raise public awareness about the conservation and protection of these marine mammals.

"It must be remembered however, that any water-based activity has the potential to cause disturbance, therefore it is vital that boat operators follow strict guidelines to lessen any impact to the animals' natural behaviour – such as feeding, resting or socialising. We believe cetaceans do not belong in captivity and seeing them in the wild is the best way to encourage respect for the species, but this has to be carried out responsibly."

Currently, Britain does not have a national code of conduct in law for approaching whales and dolphins in the wild. *Figures 1 and 2*, below, illustrate the best way to approach whales and dolphins.

We would like to give the final word to Peter Stevick, the Science Director of *Hebridean Whale and Dolphin trust*.

"Developing an awareness of the animals that you are with is central to responsible and non-disruptive wildlife watching. The difference between a good approach to an animal and a poor one has a great deal to do with understanding and responding to the reaction of the whale or dolphin."

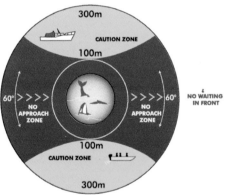

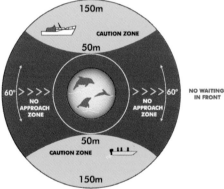

WHALES

Figure 1 illustrates the approach distances for whales. The caution zone (shown in yellow) is the area within 300m either side of a whale. The vessel should operate at 'no wake speeds' within this zone. No more than two vessels should be in this area. The No Approach Zone is within 100m of a whale, and also includes the area directly in front of or behind a whale out to 300m. Vessels should not enter the No Approach Zone and should not wait in front of the direction of travel of an animal or pod of animals. Vessels should also avoid repeated attempts to interact with whales if they show signs of disturbance. Vessels should limit their time with a single pod, and where possible stay in radio contact with other vessels.

DOLPHINS

Figure 2 illustrates the approach distances for dolphins. The Caution Zone (shown in yellow) is the area within 150m either side of a dolphin. No more than two vessels should enter the Caution Zone at any one time and vessels should operate at 'no wake speeds' within this zone. The No Approach Zone is within 50m of a dolphin, and also includes the area directly in front of or behind a dolphin out to 150m. Vessels should not enter the No Approach Zone and should not wait in front of the direction of travel of an animal or pod of animals. Vessels should also avoid repeated attempts to interact with dolphins if they show signs of disturbance, and limit their time with a single pod. Vessels should try and maintain radio contact with other vessels.

Courtesy of the *Australian National Guidelines for Whale and Dolphin Watching 2005* © Commonwealth of Australia.

Responsible Whale Watching

Whale and Dolphin Watching Holidays
UK & Worldwide plus <u>the</u> best choice of Wildlife Cruises

brochureline: 0117 9375 689
info & bookings: 0117 9658 333
email: wildinfo@wildwings.co.uk
web: www.wildwings.co.uk

USEFUL WEBSITES

Organisations
Aberdeen University Lighthouse Field Station
www.abdn.ac.uk/zoology/lighthouse
Beaked Whale Resource
www.beakedwhaleresource.com
British Divers Marine Life Rescue
www.bdmlr.org.uk
Cetacea Defence
www.cetaceadefence.org
Cetacean Research and Rescue Unit
www.crru.org.uk
Cetacean Society International
www.csiwhalesalive.org
Dolphin Care
www.dolphincareuk.org
Dolphin Project
www.dolphinproject.org
Dolphin Space Programme
www.dolphinspace.org
Friends of the Moray Firth Dolphins
www.loupers.co.uk
European Cetacean Society
www.europeancetaceansociety.eu/ecs
Gower Marine Mammals Project
www.gmmp.org.uk
Greenpeace
www.greenpeace.org
Hebridean Whale and Dolphin Trust
www.whaledolphintrust.co.uk

International Dolphin Watch
www.idw.org
International Fund for Animal Welfare
www.ifaw.org
Irish Dolphins www.irishdolphins.com
Irish Whale and Dolphin Group
www.iwdg.ie
Marine Connection
www.marineconnection.org
Marine Conservation Society
www.mcsuk.org
Marinelife www.biscay-dolphin.org.uk
National Seal Sanctuary
www.sealsanctuary.co.uk
ORCA - Organisation Cetacea
www.orcaweb.org.uk
Royal Society for the Prevention of Cruelty to Animals
www.rspca.org.uk
Sea Mammal Research Unit
http://smub.st-and.ac.uk
Sea Shepherd Conservation Society
www.seashepherd.org
Seaquest Southwest
www.cornwallwildlifetrust.org.uk/nature/marine/seaquest.htm
Seawatch Foundation
www.seawatchfoundation.org.uk
Shetland Sea Mammal Group
www.natureshetland.co.uk/seamammal

Wildlife Trusts , The
www.wildlifetrusts.org
Whale and Dolphin Conservation Society www.wdcs.org
World Wide Fund for Nature
www.panda.org

Photographic agencies
Breathtaking Whales
www.breathtakingwhales.com
Wild Pics
www.WildPics.org

Specialist Publishers
Cetacea Publishing
www.cetaceapublishing.com
WildGuides www.wildguides.co.uk

Others
Earthwatch Institute www.earthwatch.org
International Whaling Commission
www.iwcoffice.org
UK cetacean network (UKCetnet)
http://tech.groups.yahoo.com/group/ukcetnet
Whale-Watching-Web
www.physics.helsinki.fi/whale
Wise Scheme www.wisescheme.org/
Scottish National Heritage Marine Code
www.marinecode.org

SUGGESTED FURTHER READING

A guide to the identification of the Whales and Dolphins of Ireland.
J. Wilson and S. Berrow. 2006. The Irish Whale and Dolphin Group (IWDG), Ireland.

A guide to the whales, dolphins and porpoises of the United Kingdom (2000). *The first WDCS annual report on the status of UK cetaceans.* D. Walker and M. De Boer. 2003. Whale and Dolphin Conservation Society (WDCS), UK.

Encyclopedia of Marine Mammals
W.F.Perrin, B.Würsig and J.M. Thewissen (Eds.). 2002. Academic Press, USA.

Eyewitness Handbook of Whales, Dolphins and Porpoises.
M. Carwardine.1995. Dorling Kindersley, London.

Guide to Marine Mammals of the World.
P.A. Folkens, R.R. Reeves, B.S.Stewart, P.J. Clapham and J.A. Powell. 2002. Chanticleer Press, New York.

Mark Carwardine's Guide to Whale Watching. Britain and Europe: *Where to*

go, what to see. M. Carwardine. 2003. New Holland Publishers, UK.

ORCA *No. 2. Incorporating a report on the whales, dolphins and seabirds of the Bay of Biscay and English Channel.* G. Cresswell and D. Walker. 2002. Organisation Cetacea (ORCA), UK.

ORCA No. 3. The Annual Report of Organisation Cetacea. D. Walker (Ed.). 2004. Organisation Cetacea (ORCA), UK.

The Best Whale Watching In Europe. A guide to seeing whales, dolphins and porpoises in all European waters. E. Hoyt. 2003. Whale and Dolphin Conservation Society (WDCS), Unterhaching, Germany.

The New Encyclopedia of Mammals. D. MacDonald & S. Norris (Eds.). 2001.Oxford University Press, UK.

Whales and Dolphins: Guide to the Biology and Behaviour of Cetaceans. M. Wuirtz & N. Repetto. 1998. Swan Hill Press, UK.

Whales and Dolphins of the European

Atlantic: The Bay of Biscay and the English Channel. G. Cresswell and D. Walker. 2001. WildGuides Ltd., UK.

Whales and Dolphins of the North Sea.
K. Camphuysen, G. Peet, and F. Maas. 2007. Fontaine Uitgevers BV, Holland.

Whales and Dolphins of the North American Pacific. G.Cresswell, D. Walker and T. Pusser. 2007. WildGuides Ltd., UK.

Whales and Dolphins – The Ultimate Guide to Marine Mammals.
M. Carwardine, E. Hoyt, R. Ewan Fordyce and P. Gill.1998. Harper Collins, UK.

Whales, Dolphins and Seals. A Field Guide to the Marine Mammals of the World. H. Shirihai and B. Jarrett. 2006. A&C Black Publishers Ltd., London.

Whalewatcher – a global guide to watching whales, dolphins and porpoises in the wild. T. Day. 2006. The Natural History Museum, London.

DFDS SEAWAYS
JUST SAIL AWAY

NEWCASTLE - NORWAY

WILDLIFE CRUISE BREAKS

Join us on a cruise between Newcastle and Norway as we sail through the rich waters of the northern North Sea and the Norwegian fjords – passing through one of Europe's most important wildlife migration routes.

To experience and understand animal migrations, it helps to be on the move – crossing an area of ocean famous as a migration route! Millions of birds navigate southwards from northern Europe in search of warmer climes to spend the winter. Also on the move are Europe's whales and dolphins, as they migrate between their arctic feeding grounds and tropical breeding grounds thousands of miles to the south.

During the voyage we expect to encounter over 50 species of birds, as well as seals, porpoises, dolphins, and even whales! Our naturalist guides, who are leading experts in their fields, will aim to achieve the perfect blend of relaxed education, enthusiasm, professionalism and humour to help you to make the most out of your wildlife experience.

So why not book yourself onboard in a choice of cabins and join us on a cruise that will open your eyes to the miracle of wildlife migration!

As part of our ongoing commitment to nature conservation, DFDS Seaways will make a donation to whale and dolphin charity Organisation Cetacea (ORCA).

ORCA conducts regular surveys onboard DFDS ships in order to learn more about the status of these mammals and the threats that they face.

FROM
£229 PP

Price includes:

- 3 nights accommodation onboard ship (2 nights on 21 September 2007 departure).
- Welcome Briefing and Observations while sailing out of Tynemouth.
- Illustrated lecture on migration – linked to sightings.
- Dinner and breakfast while onboard.
- Professional guides in Marine Biology and Ornithology.
- Early morning deck observations and deck watch.
- Coastal voyage and scenery.
- Guide book.

Sailing: Newcastle 18/9 (3 nights), 21/9/2007 (2 nights), 6/10 (3 nights), 9/10/2007 (3 nights) Based on 2 people sharing inside cabin.
3 nights code: WILDi   2 nights code: WILXi

Subject to availability. Terms & conditions apply, visit www.dfds.co.uk/terms for details.
Telephone booking fee of £10 applies. Fuel supplement of £4pp applies. Norwegian Environmental charge of £2pp applies.

WWW.DFDS.CO.UK/OFFERS • 0871 882 0887

THEY'RE BACK!

... and this time they're here to help save the Planet

coming up:

Baja California

the ultimate whale and dolphin holiday!

Ian and Dylan's
Whale and Dolphin Adventures

www.iandylan.com

not only are Ian and Dylan committed to reducing carbon emissions, helping wildlife and supporting local communities; they still find time to eat five servings of fruit and veg each day!

GLOSSARY

Beak: The snout, or forward projecting jaws of a cetacean.

Blowhole(s): The nostril(s) of a cetacean.

Bow-riding: Swimming in the pressure wave created ahead of moving vessels or large whales.

Breaching: The act of propelling the body upwards until most or all of it is clear of the water.

Bubble netting: A cooperative method employed by some species of cetacean to catch large schools of fish or invertebrates by trapping them inside walls, columns or clouds of bubbles created by releasing air under water.

Cetacean: A marine mammal of the order Cetacea, which includes all the whales, dolphins and porpoises.

Continental shelf: A horizontal ledge under shallow water between a continental landmass and the ocean floor.

Continental slope: A region of incline between the continental shelf and the deep ocean floor.

Crustacean: From the class Crustacea, crustaceans have a hard shell and are usually aquatic. They include shrimps, crabs and lobsters.

Dolphin: Small cetacean which usually has a beak, conical-shaped teeth, and a falcate dorsal fin.

Dolphin Space Programme (DSP): An accreditation scheme for wildlife tour boat operators. The aim of the DSP is to encourage people who go out to observe dolphins and other marine wildlife to 'watch how they watch' and to respect the animal's need for space.

Dorsal fin: The upper or top fin in marine vertebrates.

Flank: The side of the body.

Flipper-slapping: The raising of a flipper into the air before bringing it crashing down on the water 's surface.

Flukes: The horizontally flattened tail of cetaceans which functions as an organ of propulsion.

Hydrophone: A microphone designed for use under water.

Lobtailing: The act of a large whale lifting its tail high out of the water before slapping the flukes against the surface.

Logging: Term applied to cetaceans as they rest motionless at the water 's surface in a horizontal position.

Melon: The bulbous forehead of some toothed cetaceans.

Nearshore: At sea close to shore.

Offshore: At sea far from shore.

Pectoral fin / flipper: The flippers or forelimbs of a cetacean.

Photo-identification: The study of animals through the passive technique of taking photographs to capture and recapture individually recognisable features.

Pod: A discrete, coordinated group of cetaceans.

Polar: High-latitude region near a pole and characterised by a cold climate.

Porpoise: Common name for species in the toothed whale family Phocoenidae. Porpoises are small cetaceans with an indistinct beak and spade-shaped teeth.

Porpoising: Very fast movement involving arc-shaped leaps clear of the water with a clean, head-first re-entry. This behaviour is generally restricted to some dolphin and seal species.

Rorqual: A baleen whale of the family Balaenopteridae, comprising large to very large baleen whales, which possess a series of throat grooves that extend underneath the lower jaw. They feed by opening their cavernous jaws as they swim along and expanding their throat grooves, vastly increasing the volume of water held within their mouths.

Rostrum: The snout of a baleen whale.

Spy-hopping: Raising the head vertically out of the water high enough for the eyes to view above the surface. The head usually then sinks below without making a splash.

Sub-arctic: A high latitude region situated between arctic and temperate regions.

Tail-slapping: Small cetaceans, particularly dolphins, are capable of lifting their tail flukes above the water and bringing them crashing down. This behaviour may be repeated many times in a single session.

Tail stock: The tapered rear part of the body from behind the dorsal fin to the tail flukes.

Temperate: Mid-latitude region, between subarctic and subtropical waters, characterised by a mild climate.

Tropical: Of the tropics. The region centred around the Equator and between the Tropics of Cancer and Capricorn. Sea surface temperatures are very warm and never drop to freezing.

Ventral pleats: Folded skin along the throat of all rorqual whales, which expands like a balloon to take in additional water during feeding.

Wake-riding: Riding on waves created in the wake of a vessel.

Whale: A large marine mammal of the order Cetacea that breathes through a blowhole in the top of the head and possesses a horizontal tail.

WiSe (Wildlife Safe): A training and accreditation s cheme aimed at operators of passenger pleasure craft, wildlife cruise operators, dive boats and charter yachts who may come into contact with large marine animals. The training of operators consists of instruction as to how to best view these creatures, whilst at the same time minimising disturbance to them.

Atlantic Grey Seal

© Alex Wilson / WildPics.org

© Alex Wilson / WildPics.org

Index

ME ➩

YEAH!

①

Even though I only live four minutes away from my school, I'm often late.

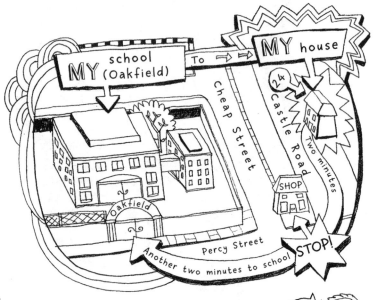

This is usually because me and Derek (my best mate and next-door neighbour) "chat" a bit (OK, a LOT) on the way. Sometimes it's because we get distracted by delicious fruit chews and caramel wafers at the shop. Occasionally, it's because I've had loads of other very important things to do.

For instance, this is what I did this morning (my first day back at school).

Woke up — listened to music
  Played my guitar
Rolled out of bed (slowly)
  Looked for socks
  Looked for clothes
  Played some more guitar
  Realized I hadn't done my "holiday reading homework"

PANICKED ○○ – thought of good excuse for lack of homework (phew!).
Annoyed my sister, Delia. Which I admit did take up a very LARGE chunk of the morning (time well spent though).
Hid Delia's sunglasses.
Took my comic into the bathroom to read (while Delia waited outside — Ha! Ha!). When Mum shouts...

"TOM! You're LATE For School!"

Run past Delia (who's still waiting outside the bathroom and quite cross now). Ignore her sisterly love.

CREEP!

Save precious time by:

 Not brushing hair

Not brushing teeth (for very long)

 Not kissing Mum goodbye

(Too old for all that kind of thing.)

Eat the last piece of toast, then grab my packed lunch and my bike. Shout **BYE!** to anyone who can hear me.

Then bike to school in about two minutes flat.

Which is a **New** TOM GATES WORLD RECORD... And this is the REALLY good bit... **AMY PORTER** has just arrived too!

I am so pleased to see her after the holidays. I smile, in what I think is a nice friendly cheery way. 😊

Amy is not impressed. She looks at me like I'm weird (I'm not).

Me smiling

HI Amy!

(This is a bad start to my day.)
Then it gets worse...

Mr Fullerman (my form teacher) makes the whole class stand outside our room. He says

"Welcome BACK, Class 5F. I've got a BIG surprise for you ALL."

(Which is not good news.)

OH NO! He's rearranged ALL the desks! I'm now sitting right at the front of the class. Worse still, Marcus "Moany" Meldrew is next to me.

This is a DISASTER. How am I going to draw my pictures and read my comics? Sitting at the back of the class I could avoid the teacher's glares. I am SO close to Mr Fullerman now I can see up his nose.

Before

NOW

Front of the class

And if that's not bad enough, Marcus Meldrew IS the most annoying boy in the WHOLE school. He is SO nosy and thinks he knows everything.

Marcus Meldrew is already annoying me...

He is looking over my shoulder while I'm writing this.

He is **still** looking... ⊙ ⊙

Still looking...

Yes, MARCUS, I'm writing about

MARCUS MeLdrew

has a face like a mouse.

Marcus Meldrew has a face like a

Moose!

Moosy Marcus...

(He's stopped looking now.)

BUT on the other side of me, the good 🙂 news is I am now sitting next to 👧 **AMY PORTER**, who is very smart and nice (even though she didn't seem thrilled to see me this morning).

BriLLIANT! At least I can have a sneaky look 👁 👁 over her shoulder for a few right answers.

I think she is looking at me |now.|

AMY PORTER is very nice.

AMY PORTER is *SMART.*

She's not looking.

She's ignoring me ... I think.

So might as well stop writing nice things now
and draw a doodle instead.

(This cheers me up.)

Marcus
gets squished by a

BIG
Monster

11

Then **Mr F**ullerman says...

"As you can see, I've changed a few things around."

(Don't I know it!)

Then he begins to take the register.

(Usually I would take this opportunity to draw a few cool pictures, or take out my comic for a quick read. But I'm **SO** close to Mr Fullerman and his beady eyes, that I have to wait until he finishes and walks to the back of the class before I can get doodling in my book.)

Ok, he's gone now. I'm thinking of names to call my band that Derek and I are in. We're not very good **YET**... but if I can think of a really good name, that will make us seem extra cool.

How about ALIEN TWINS? FOOT FIGHTERS?
I know ... DOGZOMBIES?

Mr Fullerman interrupts my drawing (I've turned the page over fast so he can't see it) and hands out the first piece of work we have to do this term. (Groan.)

Holiday Story Writing

Welcome back, Class 5F.

Today I would like you to write a story about what you did on your summer holidays.

* Did you go away?
* Did you visit your family?
* What was the weather like and where did you stay?

Remember to describe everything in lots of detail.

I am really looking forward to reading all about your holidays!

Mr Fullerman

(My holiday wasn't a great success ... but it does have a very happy ending.)

Here goes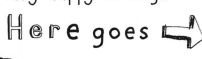

Camping Sucks

This year Dad said, "Let's go camping, it's cheap." Mum didn't seem that keen, but I've never been camping before, so I was looking forward to it.

Dad and I went to the camping shop to buy a few essential items like:

"We won't need much," he said.

1. Tent
2. Sleeping bags
3. Cooking stuff
4. Fishing rods
5. ~~TV~~
6. ~~Computer~~

Dad

But the camping shop had some cool stuff and Dad got carried away. He spent a LOT of money and made me promise not to tell Mum.

"We could have stayed in a nice hotel, it would have been cheaper," Dad said.

"Not the same as sleeping under the stars and waking up in the fresh air!" said the man in the shop as he took Dad's money.

On top of everything Dad bought ... Mum packed a whole lot more. The car was stuffed. My sister, Delia, wasn't happy about coming with us. She's not allowed to stay in the house on her own any more, because she had a **WILD** party the last time Mum and Dad went away. (I stayed next door with Derek. His parents got woken up and weren't happy either.)

We set off, and for a while the holiday was going well. Then we took a wrong turning and got lost.

LOST | REALLY LOST

Ha! Ha!

Mum blamed Dad for not listening to her properly. Dad blamed Mum for not reading the map the right way. They both blamed each other.

Grrrr

It was only when the car got a flat tyre that they stopped arguing. They phoned the Car Rescue Service, who eventually turned up.

It took AGES to fix the tyre and we didn't make it to the campsite until it was dark. Delia wasn't happy (Delia's never happy). She said the place looked RANK and she couldn't get a signal for her phone. Ha! ha! ha! I thought it looked OK. So I helped Dad with the tent while Mum unpacked the car. (Delia did nothing.)

The tent was tricky to put up, but we did the best we could.

It was a bit late to eat. Dad said, "I'll cook a big breakfast in the morning." But my stomach kept rumbling and I couldn't get to sleep. Then I remembered the secret stash of biscuits in my bag. So I grabbed them and ate them all! Crumbs got everywhere and it was very uncomfortable in my sleeping bag. Even though we had a "family tent" with separate rooms, Delia could hear me shifting around and fidgeting. It was really annoying her. BRILLIANT! So I did it some more. But at the same time I could also hear Mum and Dad ...

Biscuits

SNoring and that

was keeping me awake too. The noise was awful.
It seemed to be getting louder and LOUDER.
It was almost like thunder, deep and rumbly.
Then I realized it sounded like thunder ...
because it was thunder. Which was getting
closer. There was lightning, too, and
really heavy rain that was right
above our tent. The storm was
HUGE and it didn't take long for
the tent to blow away. AGH! HELP!

Everyone had to run to the car for
cover. The storm lasted all night long and
everything we had got wet and muddy.
Dad had pitched the tent RIGHT NEXT TO A
STREAM! Which flooded and all our stuff got
soaked.
Nobody slept at all. It was miserable.

Spot the problem...

In the morning Dad tried to get his money back from the campsite owner (as we slept in the car).

He complained a lot, but it didn't work. Mum collected our soggy belongings, which were all ruined (including the tent). I could hear her muttering things like "Proper holiday next year" and "Greece" under her breath.

Delia was crying (again) because her mobile phone had got wet and wasn't working. That cheered me up. So I decided to try and make the best of the holiday and go exploring. There were lots of interesting-looking trees to climb. I was nearly at the TOP of one, when suddenly a branch SNAPPED under my foot.

I hadn't realized how high up I was until I fell down...

It was pretty impressive, really...

Delia heard me YELP as I hit the ground.
She came over and just watched me as I rolled
around on the ground in pain holding my arm.

Ha! It felt REALLY BAD but Delia didn't
Ha! look too concerned.
Freak!

Eventually she got Mum.

24

"That's all I need," said Mum as she took me to the first aid tent. They gave me a lolly 🍭 and put my arm in a bandage (I was very brave). ☺

It looked like our camping holiday was going to be very short. More rain was due so Mum and Dad decided under the circumstances (no tent or dry clothes) we should go home. ☹

I wasn't that upset and Delia was delighted. So we all packed up and left the campsite. Home ▷

On the way home we stopped off in a nice restaurant, where I managed to eat a huge pizza with my one good arm. My bad arm was really hurting ☹ but I didn't complain because it was the first time in ages that everyone looked happy.

Our neighbours Mr and Mrs Fingle and Derek were surprised to see ⊙ ⊙ us back so soon. My bad arm was SO painful now that I went to my room to look at it.

Worryingly, it had turned purple and SWOLLEN up like a balloon. ⊙ ⊙

I showed Mum and Dad. They looked shocked. Delia said "You look like a FREAK" (which was kind of her). Mum and Dad got back in the car and drove me to the hospital, leaving Delia at home.

Luckily ... my arm's not serious. I had just sprained it, and the bandage was put on too tight. So they redid it and put it in a very cool sling instead. ☺

(I'll live, apparently.)

It was quite late 🌙 by the time we got home and there was music BLASTING out from our house. Mum and Dad were FURIOUS

Delia had invited lots of her friends round for a party and BOY was she in trouble.

I forgot all about my sore arm because listening to Delia being told off and grounded by Mum and Dad was probably the → BEST PART

of my whole entire holiday.

What were you thinking?

You're grounded!

Yeah!

THE END

It sounds like you had a very
eventful time, Tom!
Excellent work. I felt like I was
there … but glad I wasn't!

5 Merits

WOW!

Mr Fullerman liked my story! I've never had **5** merits before.

I leave my book open so AMY PORTER can see how clever I am. But she doesn't seem too interested. Maybe this will help:

I got 5 MERITS

No, she's still not looking.

Marcus says he's got five merits as well.

"Great," I say.

"We're like twins now."

(He's so annoying.)

I show Mum and Dad my story because I think
they'll be pleased with me (for a change).

Instead Mum gives me a note to give to Mr Fullerman.

Dear Mr Fullerman

We are delighted Tom got five merits. Also, can I just say that this is not the usual type of holiday we have. We are actually VERY responsible parents.

Tom's arm is fine now – in case you were wondering (and in case he tries to get out of doing PE).

Kind regards

Mr and Mrs Gates

I think Mum was worried my story made them look bad.

BREAK time!

I am catching up with a few friends who I haven't seen over the holidays. Mark Clump got another pet (but he won't tell me what it is!).

Norman Watson's not allowed to eat sweets or ANYTHING with E-numbers in because they make him go really WILD. But I can see him running round the playground with his jumper over his head shouting, "I'm a space man, I'm a space man." Which makes me think he's had a few sneaky sweets already today.

Soloman Stewart (his nickname's SOLID) is the tallest boy in the whole school. He has GROWN even more, I think.

Then Derek comes over (he's in Mrs Worthington's class, not mine, because we too much). I've seen him loads during the holidays (his hair has grown — he hasn't).

I show him my ideas and drawings for a band name. (He likes DOGZOMBIES best ... me too.)

When Marcus Meldrew barges into our chat.

"What's that?"

"Ideas for our band."

"What band?"

"Me and Derek are in a band and we're thinking of what to call ourselves."

"That's easy."

"Really?" (Marcus has an idea.)

"Yeah... Just call yourselves

'The Total Losers'.

Ha! Ha! Ha!" says Marcus.

Who's even more annoying this year than he
was last year (if that's possible).

Marcus being a TWIT

Ha! Ha! Ha!

Homework already from Mr Fullerman.
(It's like we never had a holiday.)

HOMEWORK

I'd like you all to write a REVIEW.

It could be a review of a book,
play, concert or film: something you
have seen or read.

Ask yourself lots of questions:

Describe the film/book/concert.
What did you like or not like?
What was it about?

Looking forward to reading them very
much.

Mr Fullerman

(I'll see what's on telly tonight, then read the
newspaper review. That's always a good start.)

Mr Fullerman's
SHADOW

Sitting so close to Mr Fullerman is already proving tricky for me.
Because I am being forced to ... **work.**
It's **EXHAUSTING!**

(Amy doesn't seem thrilled to be sitting next to me. Maybe if she sees me working, she'll think I'm smart?)
I will try and impress her.

She's just caught me sneaking a look at her work. I pretend to be drawing, but I've been rumbled.

I know ... I'll draw something FUNNY.

Mr Fullerman with hair...

(Amy still not impressed.)

After lessons, I meet Derek by the bike shed. Our bikes are very cool. Mine's covered in stickers and doodles. Derek's is a bit battered but *super* fast. There's a very odd-looking bike in the shed which catches our eye (not in a good way). It's covered in FUR and FLUFF with silly wobbly eyes and weird bits hanging from the handles.

"It looks like Marcus," Derek laughs.
"Or Norman Watson on sweets!" I say.
"Bet it belongs to a little new kid who
doesn't know any better!" says Derek.
"What kind of person would have a stupid-
looking bike like that?" I laugh.

Ha! Ha! Ha! Ha! We both laugh!
Ha! Ha! Ha! Ha!

But AMY PORTER is NOT laughing because it's
her bike.

School caretaker Stan is
shaking his head and tutting in a
disapproving way (which is making
his keys jangle) because I have
upset Amy (AGAIN!). She calls me an
and takes her bike away. I say
"sorry" but Amy ignores me. (She ignored my
five merits too.)

IDIOT

It's been a terrible day.

On the way home, I see posters for my favourite band, **DUDE 3**, all over the town. Even this doesn't cheer me up.

Derek does his best to make me laugh.

But all I can think about is Amy calling me an idiot (harsh) and Marcus calling us losers.

"Look on the bright side," Derek says.

But when I ask Derek what the bright side actually is ... he doesn't know.

"It's a saying."

Great.

I'll have to think of a way to make it up to Amy, which is not going to be easy.

Band practice with Derek tonight might not be so good because there's absolutely NOTHING that will cheer me up now.

Not a thing...

MUM'S BOUGHT

Caramel Wafers

FANTASTIC!

Brilliant! MY FAVOURITE!

Hooray Hooray Hooray! Hooray!
Hooray Hooray Hooray! Hooray!

(I've suddenly cheered up.)

Derek and I eat two caramel wafers each and drink some squash. (Perfect preparation for band practice.)

Mum tells me to:

"Leave one for $Delia!$"

(As if!)

Instead, I take the last one and show Derek my favourite wafer/biscuit trick.

Which goes like this:

1. Remove wafer biscuit from wrapper really carefully.
2. Eat last wafer biscuit quickly before Delia comes home (half each).

3. Carefully re-fold wrapper to look like wafer is still inside. (empty)
4. Watch Delia open the empty wafer wrapper (ha ha).

My trick worked a TREAT.

I can hear Delia moaning to Mum about me downstairs. So I take the opportunity to sneak into her room and borrow a few copies of ROCK WEEKLY for Derek and me to look at.

(Good inspiration for band practice. There are loads of good pictures of bands inside.)

We take turns to try out a few ROCK STAR POSES.

Some of them are more successful than others.

Delia's sunglasses

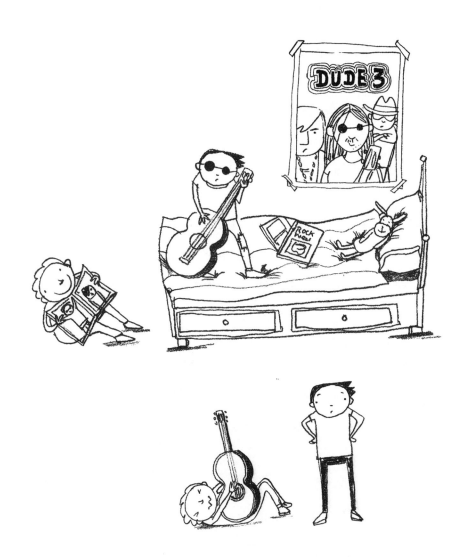

(Mustn't forget to do this week's homework — write a review... Should be easy.)

Mr Fullerman

I'm very <u>SORRY</u>.

You'll never guess what happened.

I had just finished writing my homework review when I accidentally spilt the **BIGGEST** glass of water all over it.

I am very upset, as it was a **VERY** good review. (Probably worth at least five merits, if not six.)

Oh dear, Tom!

What a mess. I will look forward to seeing it redone for tomorrow. Watch out for those BIG pesky glasses of water in future!

Homework

(I think I got away with that excuse, will definitely do it for tomorrow.)

Art

Art now ... brilliant, as it's one of my favourite lessons.

Mr Fullerman would like us all to draw a self-portrait.

These will be put up around the **WHOLE SCHOOL** for everyone to see (and laugh at, probably).

Mr Fullerman hands out small mirrors so we can look at ourselves while we're drawing (which is not easy at all).

The class are all concentrating and quiet for a change. Apart from Norman Watson, who keeps shining his mirror in other people's faces, so he's moved.

Then Mrs Worthington (Derek's teacher) comes in and takes over from Mr Fullerman, who goes off to do something more important (like drink coffee and read newspapers).

Mrs Worthington sometimes takes us for maths. She is always very enthusiastic about everything. She is being very enthusiastic now.

Hello! Hello! Lovely Class 5F!

"I'm looking forward to seeing all your lovely pictures," she tells us happily.

Because I like art and drawing, I'm working extra hard.

Amy's self-portrait looks a bit odd. (She doesn't really look like that at all.)

Hers is still better than Marcus's. He's drawn himself with a really BIG head (well, that bit's true to life).

Mrs Worthington sees I've finished my portrait and comes over to take a closer look.

"What a marvellous picture, Tom!" she says.

"Mr Fullerman will be pleased!" she adds.

But I'm not really listening to her ... because I have suddenly noticed that this close up, Mrs Worthington has something on her top lip that looks a bit like, well,

 like a ...

I am trying really hard not to stare.
(It's tricky not to.)

(Don't stare... Don't stare...
Look at her face, not her moustache.)

"Tom, why don't you do another
wonderful portrait?"

Good idea.

"Only this time, really think about
the person you're drawing. And don't forget to
put in LOTS of detail."

OK, Mrs Worthington,
I'll do my best.

Here goes...

I'm getting the feeling that Mrs Worthington doesn't like my portrait very much (or me) now.

Oakfield School
Re: Tom Gates

Dear Mr and Mrs Gates

I'm very sorry to inform you that Tom has a detention tomorrow lunchtime. This is due to an unfortunate portrait he drew of me. I do hope Tom will learn the lesson that there is a BIG difference between drawing a portrait with detail ... and just being rude.

Yours sincerely

Mrs Worthington

(Lesson learnt. Don't let teachers see my drawings in future.)

When I get home, Dad ALREADY knows about my detention because Mrs Worthington has phoned. (·_·) And more bad news — Delia took the phone call so she knows about it too.

GREAT, like the letter wasn't enough. Mrs Worthington might as well have announced my detention with a plane TOM has Detention! ✈ or a hot air balloon so everyone in the whole town knows... (Groan.)

TOM HAS DETENTION

Dad tells Mum and now Derek isn't allowed to come round for band practice tonight. AND she's making me do an extra chore.

"Sweep the kitchen floor or take out the bins" (which smell). Some choice.

Delia is LOVING this. She keeps saying

"Diddums" to me in a really

stupid baby voice which is driving

me crazy. (But I can't let her see

she is getting to me, or

she'll keep on saying it ALL night

long, and probably tomorrow and the

next day too.)

Dad gives me one of his little chats

and tells me if I don't work hard at school,

I'll end up like him. Not such a bad thing if

you ask me, because Dad's

got a pretty good job.

Chat
Chat

He has his own office (well, it's a shed in our garden) where he works on his computer designing stuff. Occasionally he gets to work in other people's offices.

Mum likes it when that happens because he has to look smarter and he earns more money.

I prefer it when Dad works at home because he has a SECRET stash of caramel wafers in the shed that I eat (and Mum doesn't know about).

So there I am sweeping the kitchen floor when Granny Mavis pops over to borrow a cookbook.

Hello, Tom! Just popping by to pick up a cookbook!

(I call my granny and granddad

because they
are both old
and very ancient.)

"You never use cookbooks!" Mum says in a
surprised way.

"I'm inviting the whole family round for
lunch," Granny says.

"Really?"

(Oh dear ... that's not really (ᵔ﹏ᵔ) very good
news. Let me explain...)

Granny Mavis and Granddad Bob are not your usual kind of grandparents.

Especially when it comes to meals. They like to experiment and eat very odd combinations of food.

pear   onion   soup

UGH!

tea   ON   cornflakes

(Saves time apparently.)

(More on that later.)

Also, Granny is just RUBBISH at cooking. So Mum loads her up with a pile of cookbooks in the hope she might actually follow a real recipe.

I'm still sweeping and trying to make Granny feel sorry for me by doing my

"sad face". Hopefully she'll slip me a bit of extra pocket money (Granny does that sometimes).

But **M**um tells Granny | why | I'm sweeping the kitchen.

Oh dear...

Rude drawing!

("Detention ... blah blah ... drawing ... blah blah ... moustache ... blah blah.")

And *now* she wants me to go to the shop to buy **Milk!** (work work work) "So Granny can have a cup of tea."

Luckily Granny gives me extra money to buy myself a treat.

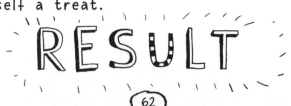

RESULT

In the shop, I'm deciding how to spend my treat money (sweets? caramel wafers?) when I spot ⊙ ⊙ this month's copy of

ROCK WEEKLY

And on the cover is the best band in the whole world. **DUDE 3**

I **HAVE** to buy it! And there's even enough money left for two fruit chews as well. **BRILLIANT!**

Mum asks,  Where's the milk?

(Suddenly I remember why I went to the shop and hide my copy of **ROCK WEEKLY**.)

"The shop had run out," I say.

(*PHEW!* Quick thinking ... must tell Derek about **DUDE 3**.)

Granny Mavis has hot water with a slice of carrot instead which is a bit bonkers even for her.

Odd

I have read the whole interview with **DUDE3**. And I can't believe that they are actually coming to play a concert *IN* OUR TOWN.

I go on the computer to listen to their latest tracks and see where else they're playing.✻

This is AMAZING. Derek is online and is just as excited about it as I am.

 Dude3 Dude3 Dude3! WHOOOOOO HOOOOOOO!!

Can't wait, DUDE MAN. Will SO be there!!!

 ME TOO ... BRILLIANT!! Can I read your mag after? Bring to skool yeh!

Spread the DUDE3 word. Dad calling, time for burnt food.

 Pretend it's fast food ... and eat it really fast... LOL!

Ha! Ha! Give it to Delia ... she won't see it with her dark glasses. FREAK!

✻www.dude3.com

Good news about the concert. **B**ad news — me and Derek are too young to go on our own. Dad will probably want to come too. Which is OK as long as I can get him to **PROMISE** not to:

1. Sing

2. Dance

3. Wear anything embarrassing

Shame

Which could be tricky because he likes to do all those things (sometimes at the same time).

I did it **MY** way

(Go back to reading my **ROCK WEEKLY**.)

DUDE 3 ON TOUR!

Rock Weekly caught up with the Dudes while they get ready to go on tour, playing all their hit songs: "Dude3 Rocks!", "Rock Out", "Fever for the Dudes". With a new album out soon, Dude3 is unstoppable!

Oakfield - The Huge Arena – 1st
Bessing Way Hall – Mon 4th
Wolfington – *Corn Palace* – Tue 5th
Colinbury – *Pyramid* – Fri 8th
Plannington – *The Arena* – Sat 9th
Bumbleton – *The Big Dome* – Mon 11th
Borem – *The Rice Palace* – Tue 12th
Sofferpool – *Pool Apollo* – Wed 13th
Cuddly – *The NIT Arena* – Sat 16th

DUDE 3

Catch the DUDE3

Hooray!

Oakfield Yeah!

Hardly slept at all last night. ⊙, ⊙

All I can think about is that

are coming to town. FANTASTIC.

Even Delia seems excited. (For her, anyway ...
it's hard to tell.)

As long as she doesn't stand anywhere near
me, I'm not bothered.

The tickets cost a LOT of money.
If I'm going to get DAD to pay for them,
I will have to be on best behaviour at all
times. This will be tough but worth it.

I'm reading my copy of **ROCK WEEKLY** in the bathroom while Delia is `BANGING` on the door outside. The crosser she gets, the slower I read, and brushing my teeth takes

AGES.

It makes me late for school again (worth it, though). So I don't bother brushing my hair, just grab my clothes off the floor to wear (they're crumpled ... but who cares). *clothes pile*

Then I stuff as much toast in my mouth as possible and take an apple to eat on the way (which is not easy on a bike).

Toast

I make it to Mr Fullerman's class with **30** seconds to spare.

Me being busy...

I'm feeling pretty pleased with myself, so I try another cheery smile at Amy, who for some reason makes a "YOU'RE DISGUSTING" face at me.

Why?

Me Smiling

Hi Amy!

Mr Fullerman announces,

"I hope you've all remembered it's your Individual School Photo today."

NO! NO! NO!

(I forgot.)

Smug mug Marcus obviously did remember. He's looking all shiny neat and new. Ugh.

I'm looking slightly more crumpled than usual due to my rushed start to the day. Oh well, never mind. How bad can a school photo be?

The whole class line up in the hall. I'm second in line after Norman Watson, who is all twitchy and jumpy.  (I really hope Norman's not

eaten any sweets.)

The photographer asks Norman to
"stop jiggling around."

(Oh dear ... he's definitely had sweets.)

Eventually (after LOADS more goes) Norman sits still just long enough for one photo to be taken.

The photographer whispers,

"This is going to be a very long day."

Then it's my turn.

Florence Mitchell  (another super-smart girl) and Amy are watching me along with the rest of the class.

I have an idea. I will try and look and all MEAN and MOODY, a bit like the photos of DUDE 3 in ROCK WEEKLY.

BRILLIANT!

But the photographer is not impressed and tells me to "CHEER UP!"

So I try and smile (a bit) ... then he says REALLY LOUDLY:

"Oh dear, you've got something NASTY stuck between your teeth."

(SHAME!)

He walks over and hands me a mirror. (Could this be any more embarrassing?)

"Better do something with your messy hair too – here's a comb."

Now EVERYONE is looking at me.

(It just got a lot more embarrassing.)

I have toast crumbs round my mouth and bits of apple skin stuck between my teeth. (Why didn't Amy <u>tell</u> me?) And now I've gone bright red too.

So much for a cool school photo. It's going to be hideous. 😕

The photographer takes my picture and I can't get out of the hall fast enough. I have humiliated myself in front of the

ENTIRE class.

Now I will be forced to hide this school photo from everyone for the rest of my life. Especially **M**um. She likes to send my school photos to <u>all</u> relatives across the

WHOLE WIDE WORLD.

ToM'S
School
Photo

There are second cousins in Outer Mongolia who have my school photos on their walls.

To Vera Gates
5 Green Lane
Outer Mongolia
The World
(Tom GATES photo enclosed)

BREAK TIME

I'm looking for Derek in the playground and I can't find him anywhere. His bike is in the shed, so I know he's here. I wonder if his school photo was as bad as mine? (Impossible.)

I ask Soloman "Solid" Stewart (the TALLEST boy in the whole

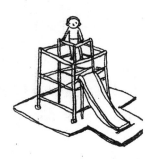

school) if he can see him.

VERY TALL

Solid points to a boy on the climbing frame.
He looks a bit like Derek, but it can't be him
because his top button is done up AND he's
got a horrible neat side parting.

SIDE
PARTING

"Mum made me," Derek says. "For the school
photo." (Shame.)

Then Derek hangs upside down on the climbing
frame and his hair goes back
to normal. Which is just as
well, because no one in

DOGZOMBIES should
ever have a neat side parting
like that.

More importantly, Derek and I chat about...

1. How **DUDE3** are the **BEST** band ever.

2. How we REALLY need to go and see them.

3. How **DOG ZOMBIES** need to practise more to become the **BEST** band **EVER**.

4. **BISCUITS** – which are better, chocolate HobNobs or caramel wafers?

5. Which biscuits to eat at band practice.

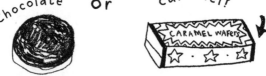

chocolate   or   caramel?

CARAMEL WAFERS

Who cares about stupid school photos?

Biscuit Doodles

Big Biscuit

WAFER

WAFER

BEST BISCUIT

AGH!

Mr Fullerman hands out our maths worksheets.

On the outside I'm forcing myself to look fascinated and interested in Mr Fullerman's sums. When really on the inside I am still reliving the humiliation that was my school photo, over and over and over again.

↖HIDEOUS
School
Photo

I wish it was the end of school right now. So to cheer myself up, I draw a few more band logos and ideas.

I'm careful to do some sums as well so it looks like I'm "working out" my answers.

A dog what's a zombie

Which one?

24 +
32
56

10 +
10
20

I am a Genius!

Marcus is straining his head and trying to look over my shoulder so he can see ⊙ ⊙ what I'm doing.

GET LOST, MARCUS...

Marcus   Marcus   = IDIOT

Mr Fullerman is looking at me now. So I put my arm right over my drawings and do a few more sums.

Marcus is LEANING back in his chair
now to see over my arm. I think he can see
my doodles, so I turn my back on him. And he
leans *FORWARD*. Then I LEAN back,
and he puts his head on the table as if he's
trying to see under my arm. Ha!

**"MARCUS ... stop trying to look at Tom's
work and concentrate on your own!"**

Yes, Marcus. NO cheating. Serves him right.

Then while the attention is on Marcus, I take the chance to have a sneaky glance at Amy's sums and memorize a few answers. (At least this way I will definitely get some sums right.)

Then I carry on with my drawings. (I'll show them to Derek later.) This maths lesson is turning out to be quite good after all.

RESULT! ☺

MR KEEN is Oakfield School's headmaster. He likes to "POP" into classes to see what we're up to.

Today he decides to say hello to Class 5F (us). Luckily I have some impressive-looking maths in front of me. (Thanks mostly to Amy.)

"Hello, Class 5F."

"Hello, Mr Keen."

Mr Keen then launches into the usual type of headmaster "chat".

While he does that, here are a few interesting FACTS about Mr Keen.

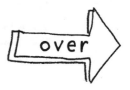

over

1. He has a very RED face that gets redder when he gets cross.

2. Mr Keen gets cross quite easily.

Here's a RED-O-METER that shows clearly the different stages of redness Mr Keen's face goes through.

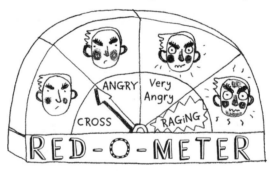

ANGRY Very Angry

CROSS RAGING

RED-O-METER

3. Mr Keen's eyebrows look like two HAIRY Caterpillars crawling across his face.

Mr Keen is still chatting when my stomach starts to make really LOUD grumbly hungry noises (it's nearly lunchtime). I'm hoping he might take the hint and stop talking. But he carries on.

When my stomach growls again I pretend it's not me by staring at Marcus.

? Marcus!

Rumble

The bell goes off for lunch but Mr Keen still keeps rambling on and on.

"I'll let you all go to lunch now,"
he says.

(ABOUT TIME.)

There's a trick to rushing down to the dinner hall without looking like you're **PUSHING** anyone out of the way. Very fast walking does the trick.

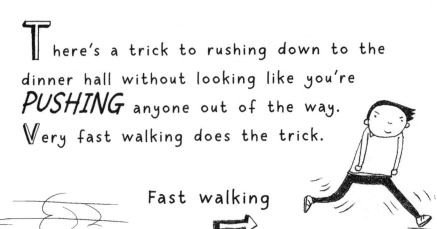

Fast walking

I grab my lunch box and try not to take in the smell of the

U.F.O.S

(**U**nidentified **F**ood **O**bjects) that are being served up.

On Mondays, Tuesdays and Wednesdays I have packed lunch. On Thursdays and Fridays I have school dinners.

This is because on Thursdays **AMY PORTER** has school dinners and on Fridays it's CHIPS.

Derek is already sitting at the table eating. So I sit next to him, and then Norman Watson sits next to me. When I open my lunch box there's a note inside from my Granny Mavis.

(Oh NO! I forgot. Granny likes to help out and make my packed lunch when she visits. And I wasn't there to stop her.)

La! La! La!

I'm really hoping that she hasn't actually tried to cook **anything** odd for me.

Looking 👀 in my lunch box, I can see something that looks a bit like a pizza.
It is a pizza.
(So far so good.)

Made in the shape of a face.
I think?

It's *my* face ... groan.

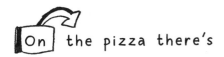 **On** the pizza there's

cheese **(OK)**

tomatoes **(OK)**

olives **(UGH).**

And something else that I personally don't think should **EVER** in a

million years be seen on a pizza ... ever ...

La!
La!
La!

(**W**hat was **G**ranny thinking?)

A BANANA!

There's a banana on my pizza.
I take it off really quickly before anyone sees
that I have a banana on my pizza and thinks
I'm weird.
Too late...
Amy and Florence walk past me and both pull
a "that's disgusting" face at me and sit at
another table.
Then Norman Watson nudges me and says,

"Is that a banana on your pizza?"

"Maybe..." I say.

"^{DO}YUM!_o I'll have it if you don't want it."

So I let Norman eat my banana and don't ask any questions. Derek whispers,

"That's gross" to me. But Norman seems happy enough, so I keep quiet. I eat the rest of the pizza anyway. (It tastes a bit banana-ish in places.)

Granny Mavis has a few more unusual surprises for me lurking in my lunch box:

Cucumber juice in a can.

Lavender and potato biscuits.

And a lemon. (Why?)

$\mathbb{D}$erek has some more normal food for lunch, which he shares with me. (That's why he's my best mate.)

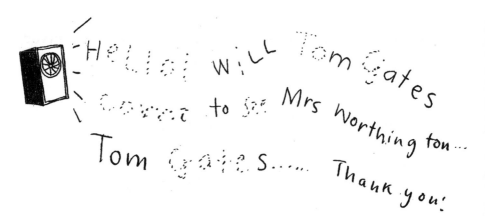

Best mate

We're just about to go out to break when Mrs Mumble (that's her real name) makes an announcement over the tannoy system. No one can ever understand what Mrs Mumble says, so you have to listen carefully.

Hello! Will Tom Gates come to see Mrs Worthington... Tom Gates..... Thank you!

I think she said Tom Gates to see Mrs
Worthington? ... She did.
I forgot about my detention.

GROAN.

I have to help Mrs Worthington put up all
the portraits we did.
(Not the one I did of her, obviously.)

When she's not looking I add a few extra
details to Marcus's portrait.

Which I think are a great improvement.

CLASS 5F SELF-PORTRAITS

Ross White

Paul Jolly

Soloman Stewart

Julia Morton

Norman Watson

Pansy Bennet

Mark Clump

Amber Tulley Green

Amy Porter

Trevor Peters

Brad Galloway

Leroy Lewis

Tom Gates

Florence Mitchell

Indrani Hindle

I am an IDIOT

Marcus Meldrew

OH NO, Mr Fullerman's been
looking in my book.

> Tom
>
> I'm sure DOGZOMBIES is a fantastic band.
> But you need to concentrate on your
> MATHS in future. (By the way, I like
> this logo best.)

> Mr Fullerman

I make a huge effort to pay attention in
lessons, as I can't afford to get into any
more trouble. Especially if I want Dad to buy
DUDE3 tickets.

Even though I know that Mum and Dad will now use this at every opportunity to make me do stuff that I really don't want to do, like:

"Eat your vegetables ... if you want those DUDE3 tickets."

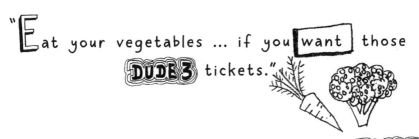

"Tidy your room ... if you want those DUDE3 tickets."

"Let your sister in the bathroom first ... if you want those DUDE3 tickets."

I can hear them now. Blah Blah! Blah Blah!

This is not going to be easy.

I'm trying to be extra good in Mr Fullerman's lesson.

I even volunteer to hand out the school trip forms.

Marcus tries to grab his form from me straightaway.

I say "**M**anners" to him, then leave him until last. Making him reach for his form a few times is fun. Until Mr Fullerman gives me one of his SCARY glares.

Teacher STARE

The trip actually looks like it could be quite good.

Year 5 class trip to the British Museum to look at **the Egyptians and mummies**.

Dear Parent/Carer

This term we will be studying the Egyptians and would like to take all the classes to the British Museum as part of the project.

This will be for the whole day and the children will need a packed lunch. We will be travelling by coach and we will need helpers on the day if anyone is available.

Please fill in the form below, which gives your child permission to attend the trip.

Many thanks

Mr Fullerman

Tear off and return to school **ASAP**.

Child's Name **Tom GATES** Class ___5F___

I give permission for my child to go to the British Museum

YES/NO ☺ _Rita Gates_ Print ___Rita Gates___

Signed _Rita Gates_
(good job!)

Does your child have any allergies? **Yes**
If so, what are they? _Do not give Tom ANY vegetables_
Are they taking any medicines? If so, what? ___Yes... cough_
sweets. Or just SWEETS would be fine

Are you able to help on the trip? ___No NoNo___

Contact name ~~~~~
Contact number ~~~~~

(All done.)

Today Mr Fullerman asks us to read out to the class our "What we did on holiday" stories. I feel happy about this because I got

 merits for mine.

It will be a good opportunity to impress Amy, hopefully.

Norman Watson reads his first.

He went to DISNEYLAND.
He's SO lucky! (But he didn't get five merits like me. Ha!)

Marcus Meldrew got sent away to summer camp for nearly the WHOLE HOLIDAY. I think he annoys his parents as much as he annoys me. (I'd send him away for the whole year if I could.)

Julia Morton's "I found an interesting shell" story is not interesting at all.

This lesson is starting to get a bit dull when Mark Clump stands up and reads "MY NEW PET SNAKE", which gets my attention.

He tells us about the mice he keeps in the freezer to feed the snake with.

And how he bought the snake, where it lives, what the snake is called (Snakey ... not very original). It's a really good holiday story.

And the BEST bit about the whole story is when he reaches inside his desk and brings out................

HIS PET SNAKE!

Here's Snakey!

Snakey!

It's awesome. But Mr Fullerman doesn't think so. Neither do half the class, who run out. SCREAMING

Mr Fullerman makes Mark put his snake away. The school office ring his mum, who comes to pick them both up. Which is a shame, because I really like snakes and I didn't get to see it properly.

At the end of school we get a note to take home.

Dear Parent/Carer

Please can we remind all children and parents that NO PETS of any kind can be brought into school.

Pets are for home, not for the classroom. Especially pets that can be considered slightly scary (like snakes).

Thank you

Mr Keen
Headmaster

Talking of pets, Derek is getting a new pet DOG. I can't wait! Delia is allergic to dogs so I'm not allowed to get one. But Derek can bring his dog round ALL the time because:

1. I really like dogs.

2. Delia will be forced to stay in her room or she'll have to go out. Either way she won't be around to annoy me.

Perfect!

Derek's Dog

Derek sends me a photo of his dog...

This weekend the whole family are having lunch at the old **FOSSILS'** house.

Mum is stressed about what we'll be eating, especially since I mentioned my banana pizza.

Dad is stressed because his brother (my Uncle Kevin) and his family will be there. Uncle Kevin seems to know a lot of things. Dad says it's because he's a "know-it-all".

Aunty Alice always laughs at Uncle Kevin's jokes, even when they're not funny (which is most of the time).

What do you call a man with no hair... My brother Frank!

Ha Ha! Ha!

Delia is in a bad mood because she doesn't want to go. I say, "Delia's got a boyfriend, Delia's got a boyfriend," which puts her in an even **WORSE** mood.

Mum and Dad say she HAS to come.

Something tells me this lunch isn't going to be much fun.

Luckily the Fossils are in a VERY good mood and happy to see everyone, which helps a lot.

Yo! kids!

Hello!

My twin cousins are already there (and eating ... they eat loads). They are even taller than Solid. I say "**Hi**" to them. They don't talk much; they just wave at me.

Mum asks what we're eating for lunch today. We all listen nervously.

Granny announces we're having:

Chicken stuffed with cheese.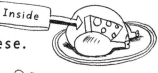

Roasted eggs?

Peas on a stick.

I really hope it tastes better than it sounds.

We're all sitting at the table when Uncle Kevin asks Dad if he's got balder, which makes Aunty Alice laugh.

Ha Ha!

Dad doesn't look too happy.

Granny steps in and asks,

"Is everything OK?"

We all say, "Yes!"

"Delicious!" "Mmmmm!"

And nice things like that. But I notice no one is eating very much apart from the cousins. And Delia is secretly texting under the table.

Uncle Kevin starts talking about their

"AMAZING three-week holiday in  Greece".

So I tell everyone about our terrible two-day camping holiday and how it rained and the tent was washed away because Dad STUPIDLY put the tent up by the stream. And then how I fell out of the tree...

Aunty Alice and Uncle Kevin seem to be enjoying the story. Ha Ha! Ha Ha!

Mum and Dad are GLARING at me in a "BE QUIET" kind of way.

Granddad changes the subject and asks me about my band.

So I tell him about **DOG ZOMBIES** and then I tell everyone that **DUDE 3** are coming to play in our town!

"Dad is SO brilliant, he's promised to buy tickets for us to see them," I say.
(Dad looks surprised but doesn't say no.)

I'm a - genius.

BEST DAD

Turns out that the cousins are HUGE fans of **DUDE 3** too. It's the most excited I've seen them since they won a chocolate fountain at their school fair.

Uncle Kevin suggests we all go together on a "big family night out". I don't mind who I go with as long as it's not just Delia. So I say "GREAT!" But Dad doesn't look pleased at all with the idea. Especially when Uncle Kevin starts going on about Dad's "terrible taste in music when we were growing up".

Dad is just about to say something to Uncle Kevin when Granny bursts into the room with...

"PUDDING!"

She has to explain what pudding is, because no one can tell.
It's a MASSIVE pile of bright pink pancakes that taste OK but look like horrid raw bits of liver.

On the way home, we stop off for fish and chips because everyone is still hungry.

Mum and Dad don't seem happy.

Delia is miserable (no change there then).

But I am VERY happy because:

1. I'm definitely going to see **DUDE 3** now.

2. Granny gave me some sweets and a pound on the way out.

RESULT! Can't WAIT to tell Derek.

(All I have to do now is ask **Amy** to the concert.)

Today I was only a tiny bit late for school. Hiding Delia's sunglasses took slightly longer than usual. Slipping them into an open bag of salad was inspired, I thought. Delia would NEVER have found them if Mum hadn't been making sandwiches.

I got out of the house before Delia or Mum got the chance to tell me off.

Just crept into class in time for registration.

Mr Fullerman looks up from the register and asks me why I'm late. I do what anyone would do in my position. Blame my older sister for locking me in the bathroom.

Mr Fullerman makes a note of my excuse in the register, then moves on.

PHEW!

AMY PORTER isn't in the slightest bit interested in my excuses because she is too busy memorizing her

SPELLINGS!

(OH! NO! NOT the spelling test.) This is <u>not</u> a good start to the day. I'm panicking and wondering how I'm going to get through this when something brilliant happens. I look over at Mr Fullerman's desk and I *think* I can see all the answers to this week's spellings test. The paper is turned over, but I can make out what the words are backwards. And copy them down quickly before anyone notices.

Like this.

(This test will be easy-peasy now!)

(What I can see.)

Bananas
Areas
Cameras
Radios
Umbrellas
Piano
Solo
Fiesta
Plastic

(What
I write
down.)

Mr Fullerman begins the test. I'm pretending to think carefully and write them down. And straightaway I realize there's a very BIG problem.

These spellings are not the same as Mr Fullerman's. Which makes me think I've written down next week's test instead.

I'm panicking, my mind's gone blank and I've missed the first **THREE** spellings already.

FOUR spellings ... FIVE spellings ... SIX-SEVEN-EIGHT ... the whole test. I keep pretending to write so Mr Fullerman doesn't suspect anything and hope for the best. **If** Mr Fullerman spots that I already have next week's test, he might smell a rat!

(cheat)

The test is over and we have to swap papers with the person next to us so they can mark them. Marcus hands me his paper.
Oh dear, I'm in trouble now..

I have to think quickly...

AGH!

Disaster has struck in the shape of a leaking pen.

Mr Fullerman makes me clean up my ink "accident". WHOOPS!

I get to check Marcus's test.
He thinks he's done very well and is looking extra smug.

Marcus Meldrew

1. potaoe ☹ ✗
2. Volcano ✓
3. Tattwo ☹ ✗
4. Kangeroow ✗
5. Hero ✓
6. Igloow ✗
7. Echo ✓
8. Mangoe ✗ $\frac{3}{8}$

Only 3/8 for **M**arcus.

Not so smug now.

Amy got 8/8 (she's so smart).

I say " WOW! Well done, Amy" (it's winding Marcus up).

"You're SO good at spelling, aren't you?"
Then Amy says, "Thanks ... but I can't draw like you can" (she actually said something nice to me).

So while the class are checking spellings I show Amy my latest **DOGZOMBIE** drawings and ask her to pick the best one. (She chooses the same one as Mr Fullerman.)

This is the longest conversation I have ever had with Amy. I tell her about **DUDE 3** and how they're playing in our town.

And it turns out that **A**my REALLY likes them too, which is **BRILLIANT!**

I'm trying to think about the best way to invite Amy to see **DUDE 3** when she says she likes singing.
I say, "I like singing too," then she says "Really?" and I say,

"**YES,** I can't get enough of singing."
So she suggests I join the school choir (like her) and I hear myself say,
"That's a **great** idea, I'd **LOVE** to join the choir."

(WHY? WHY? WHY did I say that?**)**

129

Which is exactly what Derek says when I tell him,
    "I'm joining the choir. It will be good for my singing and the band."

"You think so?" (Derek is not convinced.)

Derek

(No, I don't think so. But I'm hoping Amy will come and see **DUDE 3** and I can't tell Derek that.)

I pass a choir practice poster on the school notice board. And I can't believe rehearsals are at LUNCHTIME! I don't even get to miss a boring lesson or two.
I'll go maybe once or twice to keep Amy happy - then drop out later on.

Good plan.

HEAD LICE ALERT!
KEEP CHECKING YOUR HAIR!
REGULAR COMBING
DON'T SHARE BRUSHES

SMILE!
IT'S SCHOOL PHOTO
TIME AGAIN THIS
MONDAY MORNING
DON'T FORGET!

School Assembly

It's a "special assembly" today.

I can't believe that **MARCUS** is getting an award for his holiday homework! This seems very unfair as I got **5** merits as well.

Mr Keen, our headmaster, gives out prizes in front of the whole school.

It will be sick -making to watch Marcus being ultra smug. To make it worse, Mr Fullerman asks Marcus to take the register to the school office. Marcus thinks he's something special.

(While he's out of the class, I decide to add my own comments to his work.)

Mr **K**een is standing in front of the whole school.

He is telling us the usual sort of things that headmasters like to say.

"Lots of hard work..." "Looking forward to..." Blah Blah Blah

I'm sitting behind **SOLID,** so I can't see much of what's going on.

Mrs Nap leads the school in a rendition of "Morning Has Broken".

She is another one of those very enthusiastic teachers who *SWAYS* a lot from side to side while singing at the top of her voice.

Morning has BROKEN!

P_{ansy} B_{ennet}  (don't mess with Pansy, she's tough) and of course Marcus are both getting awards.

B_{rad} G_{alloway} (who has cool hair) is next to me. I tell him to keep his eyes peeled on Marcus.

"Sssshhhhhhh."

Mr Fullerman is giving me the beady eye now.

BEADY eyes

M_r K_{een} says,

"Today we have some very important prizes to give out. Will Treasure Alexander and Grace Cole come up and get their certificates for good work on their shared nature project."

We all clap while the girls show everyone their impressive project.

"Will Pansy Bennet and Marcus Meldrew come up with their excellent 'My Holiday' homework."

Pansy holds her book up. It has some nice-looking writing and drawings in it. Everyone claps. Then she takes her certificate.
Next Marcus holds his work up to show the school. He's parading it around so the whole school can see what's written in his book.

Everyone bursts out laughing. And they keep laughing.

(I enjoy the moment.)

Marcus takes a certificate and sits back down quickly. He's still wondering why everyone was laughing at him.

I wish all assemblies were this much fun. Because for a short time, I forget all about promising to join the choir. It's only when assembly's over and I walk past that poster again that it all comes flooding back to me...

Groan.

cross

Mr Fullerman is not in a good mood now either. (He suspects I had something to do with "adding" to Marcus's work.)

He reminds me about my review and tells us about the school concert (the choir will be singing, apparently).

And if that's not enough, he gives us a parents' evening slip.

How am I supposed to fit in band practice now?

I manage to get through the rest of the lesson by concentrating **VERY** hard on two things.

1. What I'm going to eat for lunch.

2. The small black fly trying to land on Mr Fullerman's round head.

Blah Blah Blah...

It takes a while, but the fly gets there in the end. And Mr Fullerman says,

"Glad to see you're playing such close attention to me, Tom."

Which makes me laugh. Then Amy mentions "choir practice this lunchtime".

"Great," I say. "Can't wait."

(groan.)

Mrs Nap welcomes the new faces (me) to the choir. I never knew SOLID was in the choir (he kept that quiet) and OH NO... Marcus is here too — great, I can't get away from him.

Amy looks pleased to see me, so that's something.

Mrs Nap puts me right next to Marcus AGAIN.

She begins by making us do ridiculous warm-up exercises for our voices. We pull lots of silly faces and make odd noises. Then we learn the songs for the concert. Which is surprisingly fun. I'm *almost* starting to enjoy myself.

Mrs Nap asks us all to sway from side to side when we're singing.

We're supposed to all sway together in the same direction. But Marcus keeps swaying (accidentally on purpose) into me. So I Sway into HIM. Then he SWAYS into me and stamps on my foot. So I give him a BIG shove (which gets him off my foot).

Then he SWAYS into me AGAIN so I sway just that little bit too HARD into him. And Marcus goes flying on to the floor (as if he's been hit by an elephant!).

N ow he's snivelling on the ground, shouting,

"Tom PUSHED ME.
TOM PUSHED ME!"
(He's SO annoying.)

Mrs **N**ap helps Marcus up. Then sends ME out, saying,

"**You** should know better, **Tom**. Perhaps choir is **not** for you after all."

I thought I was doing **SO** well.

I draw a picture of Marcus, which makes me feel better.

Marcus is a slimy toad.

CROAK!

HISTORY

Back in class, Marcus is sitting as far away from me as possible. (Just as well, I say.)

"**M**arcus is an idiot," **A**my tells me. She saw him push me and tread on my foot. (Maybe choir practice was a good idea after all?)

While Amy is feeling a tiny bit sorry for me, I take the opportunity to ask her about **DUDE3** . (I remember Amy LOVES the band.)

"Are you going to see them?" I say.

"**I WISH**!" she tells me. "I don't have a ticket." Then Marcus (who just can't help himself because he is a nosy twit) butts in.

"I've got V.I.P. tickets."

His dad knows someone who
knows someone who knows
someone who has got them tickets ... yawn.

I tell him V.I.P. stands for

Very Irritating
Person.

And he believes me. Ha! Ha!

So I invite Amy to the concert with me and
Derek, and my dad.
(I don't mention Uncle Kevin, Aunty Alice and
the cousins.) And she says "OK" and goes
back to reading.

"BRILLIANT," I say and that's it.

All sorted. We're all going to see my favourite band. That was easy. Then stupidly, I stop listening to the history lesson and imagine being at the concert instead (which is much more fun).

DUDE 3 are fantastic - playing all their great songs. Suddenly, in the middle of a

guitar solo, the **DUDE 3** guitarist is taken ill and has to be dramatically carried off stage.

The lead singer asks the crowd, "Does anyone know how to play **DUDE 3** songs?"

"ME!" I shout and jump on stage. The crowd cheers. Amy cheers. Derek cheers. I start to play and the crowd are amazed. They begin to call my name.

TOM! *TOM!*

TOM!

TOM!

TOM!

Mr Fullerman is shouting at me. (I've missed most of the history lesson.)

Worth it, though.

Will catch up tonight and get back into Mr Fullerman's good books by not being late for the school trip tomorrow.

Which I'm really looking forward to now.

School Trip

Mr Fullerman is not pleased because I am LATE again. It was Delia's fault (well, that's what I tell Mr Fullerman).

Everyone is already on the coach and very excited.

Especially Norman Watson, who keeps leaping up and down in his seat.

On the coach, I can only see one spare seat left, right next to...

NO, not **Mrs** Worthing"tash"!

Free seat

Hello, Tom!

Derek has already saved me a place by him. But he thinks it's funny to watch me panic.

"**Y**our face!" he laughs.
"Ha! Ha! Very funny," I say.

The coach journey takes **AGES** because some of the class need the toilet and **Julia Morton** feels travel sick (she's gone a nasty shade of green). So we have to keep stopping. Eventually we arrive at the museum.

It's **HUGE,** with big stone steps up to old wooden doors that have massive pillars either side. Lots of other schools are there (all better behaved than us).

We get split up into three groups with one teacher each (we've got Mrs Nap).

We're all given an Egyptian Quiz to do. I'm in Amy's group with Derek, so we rush round the museum, mostly copying what Amy writes. The quiz doesn't take long so we get to check out the gift shop early.

I know exactly what I want to buy.

At lunchtime SOMEONE (OK, me) gives Norman half a caramel wafer. (I forget that sugar makes Norman even more hyper than usual.)

We are all sitting listening to the Museum Egyptian Expert. She is showing us a real mummy and telling us in great **GORY** detail how the Egyptians would

"use a long hook to pull out the dead person's brain through their nose before mummifying them..."

Julia Morton goes green and feels sick again.

Norman can't sit still and wants to take a closer look at the mummy.

He JUMPS up a bit too quickly and

pushes Brad Galloway, who bumps into Leroy, who falls ON SOLID, who accidentally shoves Mrs Worthington. Then she falls over and knocks into a very rare Egyptian vase...

Thankfully Mr Fullerman manages
to **CATCH IT!**

He's holding on to it really tightly and
breathing a sigh of relief just when Julia
Morton leans forward and is sick.

(I don't think that's what Egyptian vases
were originally used for.)

The museum expert can't get rid of us
quickly enough.
While Julia is getting "cleaned up"
we all get to go to the gift shop again.
I buy some brilliant Egyptian tattoos.

On the way home the coach is much
quieter because some kids have gone to sleep.
Including Marcus. Which is excellent news
because:

1. I don't have to listen/talk to him
   (he's annoying).
2. I'm still cross he got me kicked out
   of choir practice.
3. It gives me a chance to try out
   my new "Egyptian tattoos".

Which work a treat!

I am doing some more drawing, which gets me **THINKING** about some other interesting **STUFF...**

Moon Biscuit

Rules:

Here are a few rules based on stuff that's happened to me (so it's all true).

RULE 1.

School photos are always HIDEOUS. It's the law, I think. Even if a world-famous photographer was to take a school photo, it would STILL be rubbish.

HIDEOUS school photo

RULE 2.

Your siblings (in my case, Delia) know ways to annoy you that nobody else does.

RULE 3.

Your parents get MORE embarrassing with age.

My dad is now officially the

WORLD CHAMPION of embarrassing dads.

When we got back from the school trip, Dad
was there to pick me up.
He was wearing:
A nasty-coloured bobble hat with his name
on it.

Muddy jeans tied up with a piece of string.

NO belt, just STRING.

A grubby shirt with holes and patches.

And filthy old wellington boots.

"I've been gardening," he said.
(Like that's an excuse!)
"Well, I won't bother to pick you up again."
(If only.)

Brad Galloway and Mark Clump both thought
he was a tramp.

Ha!   Ha!   Ha!   Ha!

"Look at that tramp over there," they
laughed.
"Imagine if he was YOUR DAD !"   Ha!
    Brad said.

"He is my dad," I told them. I couldn't get
home fast enough.

I only forgave Dad when he pulled out four
(slightly muddy)  tickets from his
pocket.

BRILLIANT !

(That's why he came to
pick me up.)

I'm officially excited now and very happy.

AT home Delia spoils everything by waving my school photo around and laughing at it. "FREAK photo or WHAT?"

Annoyingly, I have to agree. It's AWFUL, terrible, a really rotten, cheesy picture.

HIDEOUS school photo

I've got odd hair and a red face. I knew it would be bad, but not *that* bad.

AGHH!

I grab it back from her and try to hide it before Mum sees it. Delia says,

"TOO LATE, NERD BOY."

Apparently Mum loves it and has already ordered about a million copies for the entire family...

GROAN.

ToM'S School Photo

I tell Derek about the DUDE3 tickets. Derek tells me he's got his NEW PUPPY!! He's going to bring the puppy over to mine tonight for band practice so I can see it. (Also Delia is allergic to dogs and that will keep her away.)

Mr Fullerman appears to be in a good mood. (Despite me only just making it to school on time ... *and* forgetting my review homework **AGAIN.**)

"Today we're going to be making models of pyramids."

(Which sounds like fun for a change.)

He puts us into groups. I'm with Norman, Amber, Pansy, Indrani and **SOLID.**
(I have to move tables.)
Solid has a good idea for the shape of the model.
"It should be sort of pyramid-shaped?"
GENIUS.

Indrani draws a card template and Amber cuts it out. Then we all help to cover it in glue and paper, which makes a nice and sturdy model.

Everyone is working together really well (unusually for Class 5F). Our pyramid is actually starting to look a bit like ... a pyramid.

Mr Fullerman's attention is on Mark Clump's group, who aren't doing so well.

Then Norman starts to get bored. (He gets bored easily.)

"Let's make a mummy," he suggests.

GREAT IDEA.

Norman gets six loo rolls from the school toilet and tries to "wrap up" SOLID. But there's not enough paper to cover him (too big and tall). So we use Norman instead. He's smaller but a lot more fidgety.

"Keep still, Norman," I tell him.

It's not easy covering his legs and head with the loo roll. When he's finally mummified, Norman starts walking around with his arms stretched out (like a real mummy).

He makes  noises.

It's very realistic. He's good.

He's scaring Amber. AGH!

Mr Fullerman looks over to see what we're up to.

SUDDENLY, Mr Keen the headmaster bursts into the classroom.

(On one of his little visits.)

Norman is still behind the door. He doesn't move.

Mr Keen asks about the school trip and admires our pyramid work.

(WHHHHOOOOOOOOOOAA WOOOOOOOOOOOOOAAA)

"What's that strange moaning noise?"

The class start laughing.

(WHHHHOOOOOOOOOOAA WOOOOOOOOOOOOOAAA)

"There it is again."

Mr Keen's face starts to hover around the "getting cross" colour on the Red-O-Meter when he's called away by an announcement from Mrs Mumble. And as Mr Keen closes the door, everyone can now see Norman making

RED-O-METER

ANGRY Very Angry CROSS RAGING

WHHHHOOOOOOOOOOAA   WOOOOOOOOOOOOOOAAA

noises and pretending to be a mummy.

Including Mr Fullerman.
Who's not in such a good mood now.

WHHOOOOOOOOOOAAAAA
WHHOOOOOOOOOOAAAAA

It's been an eventful
day at school.

(Caretaker Stan replacing toilet rolls→)

I can't wait to meet Derek's new PUPPY now! He's very cute (unlike Derek), although I can see a slight similarity from the picture he emailed me.

We let him run around my house .... into Delia's room. Where he chews a few pairs of sunglasses and jumps on her bed.

GOOD DOG!

Delia is furious.

But she has to keep her distance because she's allergic to dogs.

Derek and I are busy practising some new DOGZOMBIES tunes (Derek's dog

is ~~singing~~ sorry, *howling* along) OOWWl

when Dad pops his head round the
door. He wants to know if we need
another guitarist for the band. (We don't.)

hello!

He says things like that in a jokey kind of
way. But sometimes I think he really means it.
Dad reminds us about the concert next week.

Apparently Delia's not coming with us
because she's going with "friends" (I think she
has a boyfriend, which is a horrible thought). At
least she won't be able to spoil my fun like usual.

Uncle Kevin, Aunty Alice and the twins
are meeting us at the concert. I feel
sorry for anyone who ends up
standing behind the twins. They
won't see a thing.

Can't see

Derek and I discuss wearing our **DUDE3**
T-shirts.
(Must check what Dad plans to wear just in
case it's too embarrassing. It will be.)

TOM ... where is your HOMEWORK?

Mr Fullerman is in a really **BAD** mood today.

I keep forgetting to bring in my review homework.

I'm going to get another detention at this rate.

He's not pleased at all.

Plus we have parents' evening tonight (I forgot about THAT as well).

Now Mum and Dad will be the LAST parents to see Mr Fullerman.

Because I didn't bring my form. ☹

Being last will give them far too much time to look at my work and "chit-chat" to everyone (teachers and other parents – it will be awful).

Mr Fullerman gives us today's work.

CLASS 5F _____

Today, I'd like you to write a piece about your
HOBBIES.

Anything that you do outside of school.
Sports, music, swimming, singing.
Do you collect stamps?
Do you like drawing?
Why did you start the hobby?
What does it mean to you?
Do you need any special equipment?
Have you won any prizes?
Would you recommend this hobby to anyone else?

Write at least one A4 page, please.

Mr Fullerman

Mmmmmm ... hobbies?

My hobbies are

    (·◡·) annoying Delia

    (·◡·) being in a band

    (·◡·) and eating caramel wafers.

I could write a whole A4 page on annoying
Delia, but I'm not sure that's what Mr
Fullerman had in mind.

What to write? What to write??

I KNOW - I'll make up a more
interesting hobby for me to do. Something
funny?

Good idea.

We spend most of the day sorting out our classroom and getting our books ready for parents' evening.

Marcus leaves his books out on his desk while he goes to the toilet.

(Mistake!)

I slip a few drawings I've done in between the pages of his work.

(That should make his parents' evening more interesting.)

Mr Fullerman is PIG MAN
→
by Marcus

My parents are thick

Ha Ha Ha!

Ha Ha

Mr Fullerman Is an IDIOT

PARENTS' EVENING

Mum and Dad (as predicted) are not happy that they'll be the last parents to see Mr Fullerman.

It's always a bit weird coming back into school in the evening. Especially when the classroom is all clean and tidy (not like normal).
Mr Fullerman is wearing a suit and looks uncomfortable. Dad is wearing a terrible T-shirt, so I beg him to leave his jacket on.

SHAME

Mum insists on looking at EVERY piece of work up on the walls. Worse still, she keeps talking to teachers LOVELY work! that I don't have lessons with AND parents of kids I don't even know. It's SO embarrassing! Hello

I spot SOLID, who doesn't look happy (he looks JUST like his DAD, though).

"Parents' evening sucks," he whispers.

I agree.

Then I see Amy. Her parents are with Mr Fullerman already. They are both smiling and laughing (no problems with Amy's work, then).

Dad says he's got Amy's DUDE3 tickets in his pocket DUDE3 and he could give it to her "folks" now.

(Folks? Don't say folks, please?)

So we wait for them to finish. Then Dad strikes up a conversation with Amy's dad about MUSIC in a really LOUD voice.

Amy rolls hers eyes and looks at me. "Sorry," I say, and we both have to stand there and wait for our parents to stop embarrassing us. They chat for ages about all kinds of rubbish.

Then Dad forgets to give them the tickets after all that!

Finally, when **M**r Fullerman has seen all the other parents, it's our turn ... groan.

He brings out a folder that's full of letters.

← Tom's letters

"Can I start with Tom's letters from home?" he says.

Mum and Dad look a bit puzzled.

Not the LETTERS NO!!

(I've been rumbled.)

Dear Mr Fullerman

Poor Tom has a cold and can't do sports outside ... ever.

Love from

Rita Gates

Dear Mr Fullerman

Please can Tom be excused from Spelling this week. He's had a difficult week (family stuff).

Thanks

Rita Gates

Dear Mr Fullerman

Tom has been helping his sick grandmother and has not been able to do his homework.

Sorry

Rita Gates

Dear Mr Fullerman

Tom's delayed homework was due to his
sister being nasty to him and not
letting him use the computer. We have
told her off.

Thanks

Frank Gates

Dear Mr Fullerman

Tom has been helping his sick
grandfather and has not been able to
do his homework.

Whoops

Frank Gates

Dear Mr Fullerman

Please can Tom be excused from
swimming?
He is allergic to ~~water~~ chemicals in
the water.

Thank you

Rita Gates

It's not a good start to parents' evening.
(What can I say? ... It worked for a while.)

But the good news is, I'm doing well at ART
and English.

Spelling is only so-so. Could improve at maths.
Could do better at science and history. Good
at PE.

It's not all bad.
Room for improvement, Mr Fullerman says.

They have a nice chat about me (like I'm not
there).

Chat
Chat

Tom
this
Tom
That

I smile and agree not to:

1. ☺ Chat so much. ☺

2.  so much.

3. ☺ Fake letters from home again.

Generally I'm an OK kid.

It's a *reasonably* good parents' evening.
Then Mum and Dad both read

"MY NEW HOBBY" (which I completely
forgot about). And it all goes HORRIBLY
wrong.
From the looks on their faces I can see
they're not happy.

MY NEW HOBBY

By Tom Gates

My mum and dad like to use my pocket money as an extra way of making me do things I'm not very keen on doing.

For instance...

"Tidy your room ... or no pocket money."

"Eat your vegetables ... or no pocket money."

"Be nice to your sister ... or no pocket money."

(Which I think is possibly against my human rights?) And if that's not bad enough, Dad seems to take great pleasure in placing my money on very high places. Like doors, shelves, and anywhere I can't easily reach it.

When I do finally get my hands on it,
Mum often borrows it back to buy
milk and newspapers. Emergency is
what she says. money

I discovered my new hobby completely by
accident.

Fed up of listening to Mum and Mrs Fingle
(Derek's mum) "chit-chatting" outside the shops
(for what seems like HOURS), I sit on the
pavement
and look really Chit-chatting Mrs Fingle
bored (my legs ache too). When someone walks
past me, he drops some money into my lap.

Real money!

It's **BRILLIANT!**

(I think they must feel SORRY for me?)

So I put on an even *sadder* face, and someone else gives me another £1.

By the time Mum and Mrs Fingle have finished talking, I've made £3.70 all on my own.

Which gets me thinking. What if I use a SHAKILY written sign like

PLEASE
HELP
ME

and wear some old worn-out clothes?

So I give that a go too, and sure enough I make even MORE money.

The great thing about my new hobby is you can do it anywhere and you get to meet

LOTS of different people. And now I don't have to rely on Mum and Dad for my pocket money any more. It's a hobby I would recommend to **EVERYONE.**

I am also in a band called

But we don't make any money at all (yet).

The End

"YOU'VE BEEN BEGGING?

I CAN'T BELIEVE IT!"

BEGGING!

Mum and Dad keep looking 👀 at me and shaking their heads.

(I wasn't begging; it's just a STORY.)

On the way home, they remind me again that **"NOT** everyone is as lucky as you, Tom."

And "begging is no joke!"

I'm trying to convince them that I was not begging. I tell them I was using my imagination.

I would NEVER beg. EVER!

"It was just a story! You know, pretending ... ha ha ha?"

I think they believe me now. Phew.

Delia hears Mum and Dad talking about my parents' evening and how they thought I'd been begging.

She suddenly comes over and offers me a caramel wafer. Even though I KNOW she's up to something, I STUPIDLY go to take it.

"I hear you're good at begging? Beg for the wafer, then," she says, and wafts the wafer in front of me. I want that wafer SO badly that I actually say **"PLEASE."**
And she says, **"SAY PRETTY PLEASE."**
So I say, **"PRETTY PLEASE."**

(It's so humiliating.)

"**I** can't hear you!"

"PRETTY PLEASE!"

Then, to my surprise, Delia actually hands over the wafer and goes off laughing.

It's only when I try and open the wafer I realize that I have fallen for the old "empty biscuit wrapper" trick.

Very funny, Delia.

Empty

Very funny.

I suddenly feel inspired to write a new song. When Derek comes round later I show him a new song I've just written for

DOG

ZOMBIES

He likes it a **LOT!**

Delia's a Weirdo

Who's that weirdo over there?
Dressed in **bLack**
With greasy hair
You can't trust her
She's not nice
She's got no heart
Just a block of ice

CHORUS

Delia
She's a WEIRDO
Delia
She's a GEEK
Delia
She's a WEIRDO
Delia
She's a FREAK

Delia's a grumpy moo
Don't let her
Stand next to you
Big black glasses
Hide her eyes
She really smells
And that's no lie

CHORUS

BACK at School

Tom, I'm still waiting for your HOMEWORK.

(I got carried away practising "Delia's a Weirdo". It's sounding really good. I have written a few more good verses. Will have to do homework TONIGHT ☾ *
*

before the **DUDE3** concert.)

I'm SO excited I can hardly concentrate.

Marcus is going on and on and **ON** about his V.I.P. tickets. v.i.p. v.i.p.
v.i.p. v.i.p.
"Shut up, Marcus." Even Amy is fed up with him.
Mr Fullerman reminds us that **DUDE3** is not the only concert coming up
(how did he know about **DUDE3** ?).

192

"Don't forget about the SCHOOL CONCERT," he tells us.

When **M**r Fullerman starts the lesson, I'm trying to work out how many hours it will be before the concert starts.

LOADS ... too many.

The clock in the classroom doesn't seem to be moving at all. This is the LONGEST lesson Mr Fullerman has ever given us.

I am staring ⊙⊙ at the clock and it's definitely NOT moving.

The more I stare ⊙ ⊙ ... the slower the time goes.

And Mrs Mumble keeps interrupting the lesson with announcements that no one can understand.

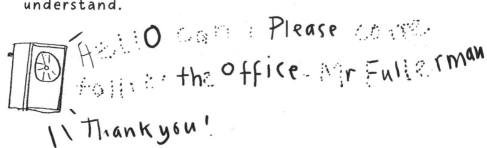

HELLO can I Please come
to the office. Mr Fullerman

\\ Thankyou!

"Did anyone understand that?" Mr Fullerman asks. Then she says it again, but it's no clearer. (This lesson is NEVER going to end!)

Mr Fullerman leaves the classroom to check what's going on. **"It might be important,"** he says. (As if.)
While he's gone, I have a

BRAINWAVE!

I stand on the table and MOVE the hands on the clock forward so the lesson is nearly finished. (This goes down well with my classmates.)

Hooray Hooray! HOORAY!

Mr Fullerman looks slightly confused when he comes back. He checks his own watch.

"Is the clock fast?"

"NO, MR FULLERMAN."

"Has anyone touched the clock?"

"NO, MR FULLERMAN."

He notices the clock is slightly wonky on the wall. Mr Fullerman is not convinced. He stands on a chair to put the clock back to the right time.

Just as Mrs Mumble makes another anouncement. It makes Mr Fullerman jump, and he wobbles off the chair and on to the floor.

It's a DISaSTER!

(We'll **never** get out of this lesson at this rate.)

Not that I'm being unsympathetic. But this is turning out to be the longest lesson EVER.

Mr Fullerman is wincing in pain and takes TWICE as long to do or say anything. And the rest of the day doesn't go any faster.

(It's like someone knows it's the concert tonight and is deliberately slowing the world down.)

MATHS is a drag. PE takes for ever. I'm getting changed out of my PE kit in the sports changing rooms when there is another really loud noise that starts

BLARING

out of the speakers.

(Not Mrs Mumble this time. Something even LOUDER.)

Mr Fullerman says it's a

FIRE ALarm DRILL!

"Leave everything and exit in an orderly fashion. DON'T RUN! Go outside."

I manage to grab my shoes and follow everyone else outside to the playground. Even though we have to **wait** for the register to be taken and wait for all the other classes to come out. Time suddenly seems to be

~~⟷~~ *FLYING* by. Mainly because Marcus has left his trousers →

behind and is standing in the playground in just his pants.

Mrs Nap gives

him a jumper to tie round his waist. ☺
Now it looks like he's wearing a skirt.

(197)

I t's the FUNNIEST thing I've seen in ages.

Mr Fullerman says we can all go home slightly early now. HOORAY!

Shame!

I'm telling Derek all about what happened to Marcus on the way home (especially the jumper/skirt bit), when he tells me he's got a proper name for his dog now.

I try to guess what it is.

"Rocky?"

"Rover?"

"Fang?"

"It's ROOSTER," he says.

"ROOSTER? That's a kind of chicken, isn't it? You're naming your dog after a chicken?"

(I suppose I'll get used to it.)

DUDE3 HERE WE COME!

CLUCK

Derek has brought Rooster over and he's running around our house looking for Delia. She's already gone to meet her friend (boyfriend, more like). Derek and I are wearing our **DUDE3** T-shirts and looking cool.

Dad is wearing another terrible T-shirt and horrid trousers. He <u>doesn't</u> look cool.

Mum agrees with me and makes him change. "And no crowd surfing," she tells Dad as we leave the house.

Change.

Then DAD remembers the tickets were in his other trousers. So he goes back to get them. But he can't find them **ANYWHERE**.

THIS IS DREADFUL.

Don't panic.

 I PANIC!

Derek is trying not to panic.
We look round the whole house. In Delia's room, my room, the kitchen.
"Don't worry, they're here somewhere," he says. He checks his pockets. The bedrooms, the bathroom. We are officially FRANTIC.
Where are the tickets?

YAP! YAP! YAP! YAP! YAP!

Rooster is running around chasing us from room to room. It's really annoying because he is barking and yapping and it's making everyone stressed.

Mum sends Rooster out to the garden. I'm checking my room again when I look out of the window and see Rooster playing with some bits of paper. The bits of paper look like they could have been...

THE TICKETS!

"BAD ROOSTER!" Derek is saying. But it's too late. The tickets are all mangled and covered in teeth marks and dog drool.

"I'll stick them together," Dad says. "It'll be fine."
But it's not fine. The tickets are ruined.

"Maybe Uncle Kevin and Aunty Alice will sell us their tickets?" Dad says.

"Don't bank on it," Mum says.

"We'll think of something," Dad says.

But I'm too STUNNED to say anything at all.

We go to the gig anyway.

"I'm never going to get a dog," I say to Derek. Which is a bit unfair, I know, because it's not his fault. I'm just really angry with his stupid chicken dog.

GGGGGGGGGrrrrrrrrrrrrrr.

BAD Rooster

Amy is already there waiting with her dad. "Let's see if they'll take the tickets anyway?" says Dad. The man on the door takes one look at the bits of ticket and shakes his head.

"Sorry, mate. Can't take these, they're all mashed up."

Just when things couldn't get any worse ... Marcus and his dad turn up clutching four V.I.P. tickets. Turns out that they now have two spare V.I.P. tickets. And Marcus's dad suggests that we could have them. (Marcus doesn't take after his dad, who seems quite nice.)

Marcus's Dad →

V.I.P. Tickets

I want to go SO badly. But my DAD says that Amy and Derek should go. "Because we might be able to get in with Uncle Kevin." I am VERY ⊙ ⊙ brave. I tell Amy and Derek that I really don't mind and that I'll be fine. Then I watch all four of them go off to the concert. (Inside I can't believe Derek and

Amy have gone with MARCUS!)

This is terrible.

Uncle Kevin and **A**unty **A**lice are waving and calling Dad. Uncle Kevin is looking particularly pleased with himself. Dad tells him what's happened and how we can't get in now with the mangled tickets. Uncle Kevin says, TYPICAL YOU! which makes Dad cross. Uncle Kevin (being a salesman) has actually sold their tickets for three times as much as he paid for them. He's very happy and they're going for dinner instead of the concert. (I think the cousins would rather have seen the band.)

Great, this is turning into a nightmare.
I'll NEVER get to see my favourite band now.
Dad sees I'm **REALLY** upset.

"Stay here, don't move," he says. "I'll get some tickets, don't you worry, Tom."

I'm SO miserable.

I sit on the floor and look really fed up. The concert is about to start and we've got no chance of seeing them at this rate.

Then I have an idea.
It's a long shot, but I've got NOTHING to lose.

I'm desperate.

I find a paper bag and I
already have a pen.

Then I get writing and
drawing.

I'm attracting a bit of attention, but no tickets as yet.

A lady walks past and says "Poor you," which is nice.

Then I'm suddenly aware of a man in leather trousers reading my note.
He's shaking his head and looking at me.

I put on an extra SAD face.

Then he starts walking towards me and there's something very familiar about him.
I'm sure I've seen him before.
Then he asks me a question.

"Is this your new hobby, Tom?"
he asks, and it SUDDENLY dawns on me who it is...

BLIMEY, iT's MR FULLERMAN.

AGH!

LEATHER TROUSERS!

AND HE he's wearing leather trousers! What's doing here? It's a terrible moment bumping into a TEACHER outside of school. You don't really think of them having a life outside of being a teacher.

It's a shock (especially the leather trousers).

$\mathbb{D}$ad comes back, with no tickets.
He's -NOT- pleased to see me begging.

YOU'RE BEGGING?

"You told me it was a made-up story, Tom!"
"It was ... I was desperate!" I say.
"Stop begging right now! There must be
another way to see DUDE3."

Then Mr Fullerman says,
**"Hello, Mr Gates. I think I might be
able to help."**

And Dad looks as shocked as me
to see it's Mr Fullerman (wearing
leather trousers).

I'm wondering what Mr Fullerman is doing at
a DUDE3 gig in the first place. And guess
what?

Turns out that Mr Fullerman actually went to school  MATES with DUDE3's MANAGER!

They are good friends.

(Mr Fullerman is NOT just a crusty old teacher after all.)

Thanks, man   No problem, nice trousers

He speaks to someone backstage who gives us all special passes.

SQUEAK!

NOW I can watch the whole gig from the side of the stage!

I would HUG Mr Fullerman if he wasn't my teacher (and wearing leather trousers).

It's the BEST view ever!

 are absolutely brilliant and I can see EVERYTHING.

I see Derek and Amy and wave. Derek and Amy wave back. | Marcus | has his mouth open like a goldfish in shock.

(It's almost the best part of the gig. Ha ha!)

Then I spot Delia in the audience. She's with her boyfriend. So I point him out to Dad and stir things up by saying he's got a VERY bad reputation around town.

What a fantastic night I'm having. DUDE 3 play all their best songs.
Then right at the end ... it gets better...

(I'll never wash again.)

I'm still buzzing when I get home.

Dad has forgotten about my begging note (phew).

He's too busy worrying about Delia's dodgy boyfriend.

I go to bed **happy** and relive the whole gig in my head. :)

This is probably the

In the morning, Delia is slopping around the house sulking and being miserable. **Grrrrrrrr**

Apparently it's all my fault because Mum and Dad want to meet her new "friend" now. (I am a **GENIUS**.)

Dad is humming DUDE3 songs at breakfast. mmmmmmmmmm

 Mum is wearing a DUDE3 T-shirt.

It's SO embarrassing (old people trying to be trendy). I can't get out of the house quick enough.

Derek and I go to school together.

He's **SO** wishing he'd stuck with me at the concert now.

Seeing Mr Fullerman again in "teacher" mode is *REALLY* weird.

The first thing he asks me is,

"WHERE'S YOUR HOMEWORK, TOM?"

"I was at the concert, sir, remember?"

Mr Fullerman says that's no excuse and I'll get a detention unless I bring it in first thing in the morning, which is a bit harsh?

(He's SO back in teacher mode.)

With all the excitement about DUDE3, I completely forget about the school concert, which apparently is

I'm not worried because I'm not in it.

(No choir, which is a relief.) Phew.

Mrs Nap is looking for helpers to put chairs out in the hall.

Helpers get to miss lessons,

so I volunteer.

All I have to do is show the little kids what to do. HOW hard is that?

We get all the chairs out when they start to mess around. I get TOUGH and suggest a quick game of musical ♩ ♪ chairs, which keeps them happy. There's no music – so I sing my DOGZOMBIES song

"Delia's a Weirdo".

Delia's ♫ a WEIRDo
DELia ♪ she's a FReAK

It's all going VERY well. The little kids all
join in and sing along with me.

"Delia, she's a weirdo!

Delia, she's a freak!" (Very catchy chorus.)
Then I sing the verse...

When Mr Keen pops his head round the door
to see how we're doing.
We all pretend to be arranging the chairs.
(Little kids learn fast.)

"That's a jolly song, Tom," he says.

"Really, Mr Keen?"

**"Are you performing in the concert
today?"**

"No, Mr Keen."

**"Why not? You should be! I'll have a
word with Mrs Nap to give you a slot
at the end."**

"No, Mr Keen, it's fine... Really, I don't want
to sing."

"Nonsense, that sounded excellent. Don't you agree, children?"

And all the little kids cheer and say,

"YES!"

Groan ... that's ALL I need.

This could be very humiliating.

CORRECTION. It WILL be very humiliating.

Fool

I don't think Mr Keen heard all the lyrics 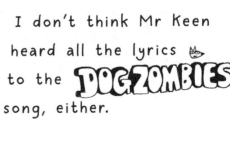 to the **DOGZOMBIES** song, either.

"ARE YOU MAD?

Of course I DON'T want to play in the school concert!" Derek says.

NO WAY!

He thinks **DOGZOMBIES** have to plan their first gig very carefully.

(In other words, we're still a bit rubbish and need more practise.)

BUT he does come up with a **BRILLIANT** plan that will get me off the hook and save me from serious humiliation.

The ONLY good thing about the school concert is we get to go home early to "prepare". (Eat caramel wafers, in my case.)

Mum says, "What do you mean there's a school concert tonight?"

(I forgot to tell them.)

"And you're in it?"

"Sort of..." I say.

Mum and Dad planned to meet Delia's dodgy "boyfriend" tonight.

"I'm not leaving them here on their own," Dad says. "They'll both have to come to the concert too."

Ha Ha! Delia will be delighted!

"I hate you"

A romantic night out ...
at my school concert.

She'll be so cross it's almost worth being
in the concert for.

Derek and I run through our plan one last
time on the way back to school.

It has to work or I'll be stuffed.

Back at school, the hall is already packed
with people. Mum and Dad sit at the back,
which is a relief because Mum has on her
DUDE 3 T-shirt and Dad
is wearing gardening gear. ← Patches

Delia and her "boyfriend" look jolly
(NOT).

Derek and I run through our plan one last
time (I hope it works).

226

The lights go down and the concert begins.
First, there's some (slightly boring) poetry.

The star was bright.
We got a big fright.
That night.

Then we have to sit through some songs

and of course the choir.
Watching Marcus and
Solid SWAYING from side
to side is hilarious.

Amy is very good (of course).

Swaying

AMY

There's a play by Year
Three. (Quite funny.)
And a dance by Year Six.

(It's rubbish.)

Then Mr Keen makes a speech about what a good term it's been

         blah blah blah.

And I hear him telling EVERYONE how he heard me singing and thought I should be in the concert.

It's AWFUL ... I can feel myself getting nervous and sweaty.

Now it's my turn.
Mr Keen asks me what my song is called.

"Delia's a Weirdo," I say.

Which makes everyone laugh ... apart from Delia, who's giving me the EVILS.

I sit on the stage and clear my throat.
Everyone is looking at me and waiting.

So I clear my throat again ...

and wait ...
and wait ...

and strum a little (like I'm warming up).
(Mr Keen is glaring at me now.)
So I'm thinking I might have to actually
start singing if Derek's plan doesn't work...

When at long LAST...

A VERY Loud BLARING NOiSE goes OFF

Mr Fullerman tells everyone not to panic.
It's just the

FIRE ALARM!

We all have to leave the
hall straightaway.

The concert is abandoned.

RESULT!

Derek is a **GENIUS!** He gives me a THUMBS UP as we leave school.

Better still ... Delia can hear some little children singing my song...

DELIA She's a weirdo DELIA She's a FREAK!

She's not happy but her boyfriend is laughing ... he won't be her boyfriend for long at this rate!

What's funny!

Mum and Dad think it's a shame I didn't get to do my song. (I don't!)

"Maybe next time, don't write about your sister, though," Mum tells me. "It only upsets her." (EXACTLY!)

Dad suggests writing about someone else who annoys me instead.

"Like Uncle Kevin,"  he adds.
Which makes me laugh.

But Mum is giving him the EVILS now.

(Uh-oh!)

When we get home, Dad and I escape to his shed to eat his secret stash of caramel wafers. (TREAT!)

Itt's the last day of term tomorrow. So I MUSN'T FORGET.

I only have tonight to finish my review homework. (It's the last piece I have left to do.)

I know, I'll review the school concert. That won't take long!
Just eat the last wafer biscuit and wrap it up for Delia first... Ha ha!
And draw a few more pictures.

THHEN I'll start my homework...

.......in the morning.

(I'll have **LOADS** of time
to do it if I get up early tomorrow.)

This is a good idea

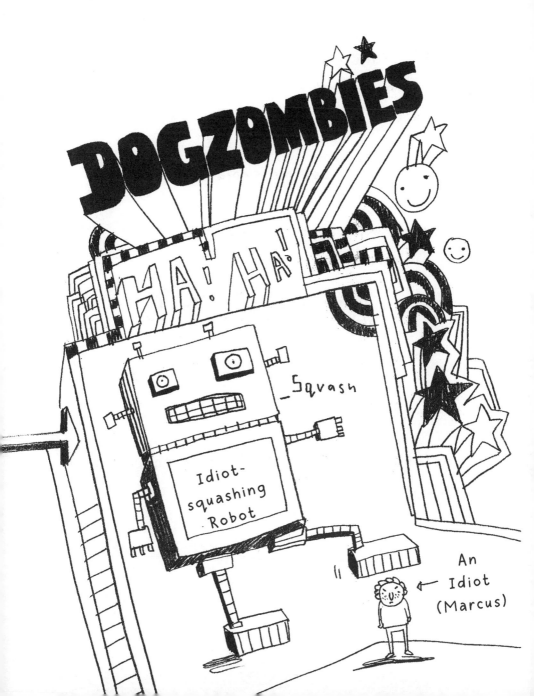

Mr Fullerman, I'm SO sorry about my REVIEW homework.

As you can see I DID do it.

Let me explain.

I was on my way to school when I was followed and

AttAcKED

by a VICIOUS dog.

I defended myself with the only thing I could think of.

My exercise book.

LUCKILY I survived (just).

But my REVIEW HOMEWORK didn't...

Sorry again...

Oh dear, Tom.
I was looking forward to finally
reading it.
You will just have do it again over
the holidays.
In the meantime let's hope you don't
get abducted by aliens
or attacked by GIANTS.
What an eventful life you have.
See you (and your homework) next
term.

Mr Fullerman

(Result!) ☺

Dog drool

My Review
By Tom Gates

Vicious teeth marks

More dog drool

The End

Turn over for something nicer

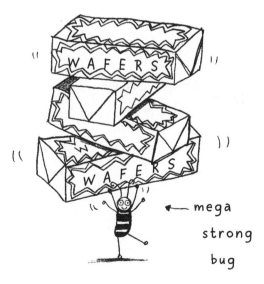

How to draw my grumpy sister Delia

1.  ← Draw this shape.

2. 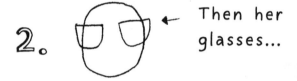 ← Then her glasses...

3.  ← Colour them in.